Teaching Organization Theory

An Instructor's Manual
to Accompany
Images of Organization
and
Creative Organization Theory
A Resourcebook

GARETH MORGAN

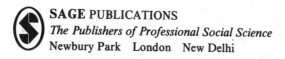

SAGE PUBLICATIONS
The Publishers of Professional Social Science
Newbury Park   London   New Delhi

CONTENTS

I. INTRODUCTION

In these notes I wish to share some ideas on how Images of Organization (referred to as Images) and Creative Organization Theory (referred to as COT), can be used to teach courses in the general area of organization and management theory/organizational analysis. They draw on my experience in teaching courses at a variety of levels - undergraduate, masters and doctoral, and present an approach that has great flexibility in that it can be adapted to suit the needs of a variety of audiences.

The basic premises on which I build are as follows:

1. I think that the courses we teach should be interesting, challenging and fun, and directly relevant to the needs of those being taught. My materials have been developed with these aims in mind. They provide a flexible resource that can be used to capture the interest and imagination of students and managers in a variety of fields.

2. I believe that the primary role of any teacher must be to stimulate thinking about the subject being taught. In teaching organization and management, this means that we must combine the task of communicating important information and ideas with that of helping students to think for themselves. In particular, I think it important to help students learn to see and analyze organizations through different "lenses" or perspectives (the skills of "reading", framing and re-framing), and how to integrate the perspectives thus obtained. This is the basic theme of Images, and one that can be adapted to suit the needs of students at a variety of levels. (For those who are interested in the details of my pedagogy, I have explored these ideas in greater depth in a paper called "Teaching MBAs Transformational Thinking", in K. Cameron and R. Quinn's Paradox and Transformation (Ballinger, 1988.) At the simplest level, if you are teaching courses that need to give recognition to how structural, cultural, political and other forces within an organization are intertwined, you will find much that resonates with your needs in this manual and accompanying resources.

3. Finally, I have a view on the micro/macro split that has dominated university teaching on organization and management over the last twenty years. I find it unduly constraining, since all aspects of organization ultimately stem from the individual thoughts and actions of members of

the organization. This becomes increasingly obvious as we recognize the cultural and political dimensions of organization: it is impossible to study these aspects without some integration of micro and macro perspectives. Thus though I often teach "macro courses" I prefer to stress the links between micro and macro issues whenever possible. However, regardless of preference, I hope that readers teaching "macro", "micro" or integrating the two will all find that they can use the approach presented in this manual and accompanying books to produce exciting courses.

In the remainder of these notes, I discuss how I implement my approach, with illustrations relating to the course outline on Organization Theory/Organizational Analysis presented in the next section of this manual. I have used this outline to teach at undergraduate, masters and doctoral levels, modifying the approach and selection of readings for the group at hand. In presenting my approach I am thus going to discuss some generic ideas, on the assumption that you will adapt them to meet the special requirements of the group that you are about to teach.

For most practical purposes, especially with regard to how this manual is to be used, the main question that will have to be addressed is whether one wishes to teach a course with an emphasis on theory or practice. I teach both kinds. With doctoral students and certain master's courses a theoretical emphasis may be appropriate. With MBAs, undergraduates and managers a more practical slant will be relevant. Using the same basic outline and approach, I vary content and style of teaching to achieve my aims. In theoretical courses I focus on the themes discussed in my class plans very directly, supplementing my basic reading list with primary sources relating to the different perspectives to be explored. (These references are highlighted in the bibliographical notes of Images, and can be selected according to the issues that you wish to emphasize). In more practically oriented courses I usually build around a case study approach. The CASENOTES section of this manual provides concrete guidance on how this can be done. So in reviewing my course outline and teaching style, please bear this flexibility in mind, and feel free to adapt the approach to achieve your own aims and objectives.

II. SUGGESTED COURSE OUTLINE

This is the outline that I use as a basic structure for organizing my courses. It follows the chapter format of Images, and needs to be adapted to suit the length and style of the course being taught. The one I have provided relates to the core MBA course in organization theory/analysis that I have been teaching for the last few years. It runs for one semester, comprising thirteen three-hour classes.

As you will see the course outline comprises a number of parts.

The first provides a general introduction and statement of course objectives.

The second provides a week by week summary of class themes, reading and case assignments. I have provided a comprehensive set of readings and case assignments that references all relevant materials in Images and COT. Remember that in designing your course you will have to select from these according to your needs. The information that I provide in discussing detailed class plans and in the teaching notes on cases and exercises will help you to make an appropriate selection.

The third provides an outline of a course project assignment: a case study in organizational analysis in which the students are required to put the ideas discussed in class into practice, by applying them to an organization in which they work, or with which they are familiar. The assignment provides the basis for most of their course grade. The details of this particular project are designed to maximize the learning for people who have some organizational experience. Other projects can be designed for students who have no real work experience, or where the aims of the course are more theoretical. For example, one can use the cases presented in COT as the basis for written assignments, or get students to conduct projects investigating the relevance of different metaphors for organizational analysis.

ORGANIZATION AND MANAGEMENT THEORY/ORGANIZATIONAL ANALYSIS

INTRODUCTION

This course builds around a series of class sessions designed to show how we can understand organizational behaviour through the medium of different images of organization. Each image draws attention to significant aspects of the process of organizing, and provides a distinctive means of understanding and managing organizational situations. The course is designed to show how managers, human resource development staff, or any other organizational member can use these images of organization as tools for informing and guiding action.

OBJECTIVES

The course has two objectives. First, to provide students with a systematic and critical understanding of organizational theory and research and the factors involved in the functioning and analysis of complex organizations. Second, to show how these ideas can serve as practical tools for the analysis and management of organizational situations. The topics covered in the course have been chosen to allow the student to analyze the organizational context in which he or she finds him or herself, both to aid understanding, and to provide an improved basis for action.

COURSE GRADES

(a) These will be determined according to performance on a practical case study in organizational analysis (see case study description), and on contributions to class discussion.

(a) Interim report: 40%
(b) Final report: 40%
(c) Class Participation: 20%

TEXTS

Images of Organization   (Images)
Creative Organization Theory (COT)

COURSE OUTLINE*

Theme 1   Understanding Organization and Management

Sept. 8   Management as a process of thinking, analyzing and acting. Images as metaphors of organization. How different images can help us understand and manage organization in different ways.

Relevant Readings

Images, Chapters 1 & 10
COT #1-21

Relevant Cases and Exercises

Eagle Smelting COT #76

Theme 2   Mechanical Images of Organization

Sept. 15   A review of approaches to organizational analysis which implicitly assume that human beings behave, or should behave, as parts of a machine. Taylor's "scientific management" and the work of so-called "classical theorists" will be given special attention. Mechanical approaches to organization result in bureaucracies, which implement a "functional rationality".

Relevant Readings

Images, Chapter 2
COT #22, 23, 24, 25, 26

Relevant Cases and Exercises

COT #74, 75, 77

Theme 3   Organismic Images of Organization

Sept. 22   A review of approaches to organizational analysis which
and   view organizations and their members as need-fulfilling
Sept. 29   organisms. Many organizational problems from this

*Instructors: Please select the items you wish to use from COT from those suggested; the items shown here reference all relevant materials; you may not wish/or have time to use them all. Add the names of the readings and cases alongside relevant COT # to avoid confusion.

point of view hinge on understanding the organization
as an "open system". This approach results in a
"contingency theory of organization", emphasizing the
importance of achieving an appropriate fit between
organization, environment and employee needs.

Relevant Readings

Images Chapter 3
COT #27, 29, 30, 31, 32, 33, 34, 35, 36, 37, 38

Relevant Cases and Exercises

COT #78, 79, 80, 81

Theme 4 Organizations as Brains

Oct. 6 A review of approaches to organizational analysis which
view organizations from an information processing
perspective. The thrust of this perspective is to
advocate the importance of learning, and the
development of self-designing organizations.

Relevant Readings

Images Chapter 4

COT #28, 39, 40, 41, 42, 43, 44, 45, 46, 47, 48

Relevant Cases and Exercises

COT #49, 82, 83, 84

Theme 5 Organizations as Cultures

Oct. 13 A review of approaches to organizational behaviour
and which attempt to understand how individuals construct
Oct. 20 the reality of organizational life. Organization from
this point of view does not exist in any concrete
sense; it rests in the precarious web of
interpretations and meanings through which humans
sustain a semblance of order in their day to day
interactions. "Culture" stands as a metaphor for
capturing the nature of organization as a network of
shared meaning.

Relevant Readings

Images Chapter 5
COT #16, 40, 50, 51, 52, 53, 54, 55, 56, 57

Relevant Cases and Exercises

COT #85, 86, 87, 88, 89, 91

Theme 6   Organizations as Political Systems

Oct. 27   A view of organizations as systems of political
and   activity. This perspective emphasizes the importance
Nov. 10   of understanding the interplay between interests,
           conflict and power in the work situation.

Relevant Readings

Images   Chapter 6
COT #57, 58, 59, 60, 61, 62, 63, 64, 65

Relevant Cases and Exercises

COT #90, 91, 92, 93, 94, 95, 96, 97, 98, 99, 100, 101,
102, 103, 104, 105, 106, 107, 108, 110

NOV.2-6   READING WEEK - NO CLASS

Theme 7   Organizations as Psychic Prisons

Nov. 17   A review of how people become trapped in ways of
           thinking and acting that often cause problems - for
           themselves as individuals, and for organizations and
           society.

Relevant Readings

Images   Chapter 7
COT #66, 67, 68, 69

Relevant Cases and Exercises

COT #88. Also see detailed class plans in this manual.

Theme 8   Organization as Flux and Transformation

Nov 24   A brief look at the deeper "logics of action" that
           underpin the dynamics of organization and society.

Relevant Readings

Images   Chapter 8
COT #19, 35, 70, 71

Relevant Cases and Exercises

See the class plan in this manual for details.

Theme 9   Organization as a process of social domination

Dec. 1st. A review of approaches to organizational behaviour
           which focus on the way organizations exploit their
           employees, their environment, and the wider society.
           This perspective has much relevance for understanding
           the conflicts underlying the problems of modern
           industrial relations.

           Relevant Readings

           Images   Chapter 9
           COT #23, 25, 26, 56, 69, 70, 71, 72, 73, 75

           Relevant Cases and Exercises

           COT #98, 107, 109, 110

Theme 10   Integration and Overview: The Art of Organizational
           Analysis

Dec. 8   This class brings the course together, emphasizing the
           importance of being able to analyze and "read"
           organizations, and to approach organization and
           management creatively - we organize as we imaginize!

Relevant Readings

           Images   Chapters 10 and 11.

Case Study in Organizational Analysis

The purpose of this case study is to create an opportunity to use the ideas and concepts discussed in class and in the readings in the analysis of a real organizational situation. The situation may be drawn from your own experience, or from some public event on which information is readily available in newspapers, reports, etc.. Your choice of situation will be an important one, and will call for considerable judgement and discretion on your part in deciding whether it is feasible to use it for the purposes of the case study. Be sure to maintain a professional stance in relation to matters which are sensitive and confidential, and disguise the source of your project (unless it is drawn from public records) through use of appropriate pseudonyms. Confidentiality and the general conduct of the project is entirely _your_ responsibility, so proceed with caution and great care.

In essence, the case study invites you to do the following:

(a) Identify an organizational situation for the purpose of analysis (the situation must be sufficiently complex to generate enough material to satisfy the specifications described below).

(b) Consider how the images, concepts and general ideas discussed in class, help to make sense of the situation.

(c) Write up as a case study in a way which relates evidence to theory, to provide an appropriate analysis and explanation of the situation described.

Successful organizational analysis rests in an ability to examine an organization/organizational situation so that its fundamental characteristics are made clear. It is not simply a question of spotting problems and applying appropriate solutions. Rather, it hinges on questions such as: What is going on in the situation that I am analyzing? How can I account for its characteristics and the way they're changing? In short, how can I make sense of the situation and arrive at an interpretation which allows me to say something concrete about it? Organizational analysis involves a process of thinking about a situation, constructing and reconstructing it in different ways that seem consistent with its nature, so that one can say something that may provide a basis for intelligent action. If the analysis has been done well, then the course of action, which is appropriate for managing or changing the situation, will become apparent.

In this course, we will be examining a number of different ways of viewing organizations. Each way provides a "lens" that highlights different aspects of organization. These different lenses may apply with varying effect to the situation you are studying - just as a particular set of spectacles may allow you to see a situation more clearly than others. Your task is to attempt to view through the different lenses and decide which, if any, are appropriate for making sense of the situation with which you are dealing.

The first few weeks of the course will involve learning to see through the different lenses, and gaining familiarity with the organization you are studying. Next will come the task of making some determination of the relevance of these different perspectives for explaining the situation. Third will come the task of writing the results of your analysis on paper, in a way that allows the reader to see and understand the nature of the situation you have been studying.

Formal Requirements:

1) A preliminary report: The aim of this report is to get you started on the case study at an early stage, and to get you into a frame of mind which is analytical in the sense that it is constantly attempting to create a diagnostic reading relating theory and practice, taking the ideas discussed in the class and applying them to the situation being studied. (See Chapter 10 of Images of Organization for an example). This report should be no more than 15 double-spaced typewritten pages and include the following:

1) A brief account of the nature of the situation being investigated, providing sufficient information for the reader to understand the nature of the organization and its context. For example, it is appropriate to provide brief information on the age, size and history of the organization, the product or services it provides, and the general nature of its environment. The purpose of this is to orient the reader, so that he or she can acquire an understanding of the industry or sector of the economy or society with which you are dealing, and the general trends it is facing. It is a good idea to do this as soon as you have selected a situation for analysis, preferably after the first week of class.

2) A series of sections applying each of the perspectives discussed in class to the case situation. Each class will give an image or metaphor through which you can see and understand the organization you are studying. It is your job to try and apply these ideas in practice, identifying the detailed ways in which the different metaphors relate to your particular organization. One useful way of doing this is to keep a course journal. After each class, ask yourself the question: How does this metaphor relate to the

organizational situation which I am studying? Take the ideas which you have been given, and sketch them on the left-hand side of a sheet of paper. Then use the right-hand side of this sheet to demonstrate where and when they apply in the situation being studied. This attempt to link theory and practice provides the basis for each stage of analysis. Each week you should be able to write a section of your preliminary report showing the relevance of the metaphor under consideration. By the time that you are required to submit the preliminary report, you will thus have already performed most of the difficult work.

Make sure that the report is written in a professional manner. It will be judged according to the quality of analysis and presentation, in accordance with the criteria listed later in this set of guidelines. The report is due on November 10, 1987.

2) The Final Report: The purpose of this report is to produce a professional analysis of the situation being studied. The preliminary report will have given you an opportunity to explore the situation from different points of view. You are now required to (a) present the situation you have studied as a 5 or 6 page case description (similar to the case description of Multicom on pages 322-325 of Images of Organization), followed by (b) your analysis of the situation - the critical evaluation illustrated in the Multicom case)

The report should not exceed 15 double-spaced type-written pages.

It is my experience that the different metaphors which we discuss in class fit different situations with different effect. Which metaphor, or combination of metaphors best accounts for your situation? In the preliminary report you had the luxury of being able to hedge your bets by looking at the same situation from a number of different points of view. In the final report, I expect you to use the insights which have emerged from this process to produce the best analysis or "story-line" that you can (See Chapter 10 of Images of Organization). This will call upon your ability to use your data and to judge its significance. For example, you may find that your case is best understood as a situation of organizational politics, one of classic bureaucracy, or one which is best understood in terms of the inability of the organization to adapt to its environment. Only time will tell. You cannot make this judgement now-you will have to wait until you have finished the preliminary analysis. If you are successful in this final stage of the project, you will find that you have a much deeper understanding of the situation studied than you did at the beginning of the course. Your task in writing the final report is to communicate this understanding to the reader. Whereas in the preliminary report you have been asked to write within a structure that requires you to apply each of the metaphors discussed in class to the case, this is not a requirement for the final report. If the idea of viewing organizations through metaphor has served its purpose, the metaphors will have generated useful insights. Your task now is to use these in any way you can, to generate a convincing analysis of the case - hopefully, one that will have important action implications. The criteria for evaluating this report, which are the same as those applying to the interim report, are provided later. The final report must be submitted by December 8, 1987.

Criteria for evaluating the reports.

The following criteria will be used to evaluate the preliminary and final reports:

(a) The professionalism with which the report is presented.

(b) The comprehensiveness and care with which the case situation being analyzed is described.

(c) The complexity of the case (cases that are very simple and offer little challenge will not necessarily earn a high grade).

(d) Demonstrated understanding of relevant theories and concepts which can be used to explain the case situation; a discussion of alternative ways of viewing the case will be particularly valuable when relevant.

(e) The quality of discussion linking theory to data, i.e. the convincingness of your analysis and general conclusions.

3) Class Presentations.* At the end of the course, a number of students will be invited to make presentations on their case studies. Each presentation will begin with a ten-minute presentation of the case situation, followed by an invitation to the class to engage in analysis. The aim of these case studies is to provide further illustrations of how theory can be put into practice.

---

*Note to instructors: This is a great way of developing skills in organizational analysis.

III. DETAILED CLASS PLANS

In order to convey the logic and approach adopted in the course as a whole, I am providing a detailed summary of how I deal with the issues presented in the course outline. Since the way in which the course is introduced to students is particularly important in developing an appropriate atmosphere, I will describe my introductory class in detail.

THEME 1: UNDERSTANDING ORGANIZATION AND MANAGEMENT

In teaching the introductory class I have a number of objectives:

(a) To show how our understanding of organization and management is always shaped by hidden assumptions that shape the way we see, understand and act in relation to problems of organization and management.

(b) To suggest that these understandings are metaphorical, and that in appreciating this, we can open the way to new ways of seeing, understanding, and acting.

c) To illustrate this concretely through means of a case study.

(d) In achieving the above, to show the transformative potential of the course: I am able to make a "money back" guarantee that the course will transform the way students see and understand organizations, and in the process provide a concrete tool for understanding and managing organizations in practice.

Here's how the class unfolds:

1. Introduction (15-30 minutes);
2. The Eagle Smelting Case Study - COT #76 (60 Minutes).
3. Discussion of aims and objectives of course (30 minutes).
4. Discussion of detailed course outline and course requirements (30 minutes).

After the personal introductions, during which I will have introduced myself and given a very brief description of how this is a course designed to improve one's understanding of organization and management, I move immediately to the case study.

I usually say that "this course is about putting theory into practice, so let's get to work." I invite students to read the

Eagle Smelting case, to spend ten minutes or so addressing the question "How would I make sense of what is happening in this case?" and then to discuss it with their neighbour, with a view to reporting their views back in a general class discussion. I allow the "neighbourhood discussions" to run as long as there seems interest and energy in the class, since it is important that they have a full opportunity to exhaust their opinions on the case before I intervene. I then conduct a class-wide discussion, recording all their views on the blackboard. (Full instructions on running this case are provided in the teaching notes on the Eagle Smelting case. I have also described the approach in my paper "Teaching MBA's Transformational Thinking," referred to earlier.)

No prior explanation of the purpose of the case is given, since the aim is to reveal some of their hidden assumptions about organization and management - the assumptions that they are bringing to the course! (Refer to the teaching notes for details). Basically, the case should be used to bring out two important points.

(a) The frame of reference that class members bring to the class and use to analyze management situations. In my experience they often favor a mechanistic model based on classical management principles, or adopt a "human relations" view of the situation. They also sometimes recognize the role of personalities, and of political conflicts.

(b) To illustrate competing interpretations of the case, e.g. a rational organization experiencing problems of communication, job design, etc., or a politicized organization underpinned by all kinds of personal conflicts.

In my experience, discussion of this case usually follows a similar pattern. The class members usually focus upon the case as presenting a problem to be solved, and proceed to identify organizational problems associated with the rational or mechanistic model of organization. They typically identify problems with communications, job design, the line of command, definitions of responsibility and authority, defective managerial styles, poor human relations and bring in other ideas and explanations that they have learned through introductory management courses, or their general experience of organization.

This is their favored way of "reading organization," and this reading shapes how they will begin to frame and solve the problems presented by the case. Eagle Smelting is typically viewed as an organization that could and should function rationally, and all kinds of rational solutions are prescribed to remedy the perceived problems. I record all these comments with regard to the rational model on a separate blackboard, using other boards to record "political" or other interpretations of the situation. For example, someone in the class usually talks about "personality conflicts" or other "feelings of injustice," or suggest that the various characters are in competition with each other for career or other purposes. The usual result of class discussion is that we have a long list of factors on the "rational" board, and just a few on the others. I will have been careful to ensure that every comment made by the class has been recorded.

When the class has exhausted its ideas, I begin to take a proactive role in getting them to reflect on the assumptions that underpin their analysis and their taken for granted view of organization. Discussion usually brings out the fact that they have a coherent image of organization that shapes all that they see. I typically ask if they can identify differences between the factors recorded on the different blackboards. Dichotomies such as the following are then usually identified in discussion:

> Rational vs Irrational
> Structure vs People
> Formal vs Informal
> Technical vs Social
> Ideal vs Reality

The class usually identifies the left-hand side as desired characteristics, and the right-hand side as the reality of organizational life - they recognize the gulf between theory and practice. I then usually pose the question: "What if you solved all the rational problems (i.e. the job design, lines of communication, etc.)? Would this organization work in a smooth rational manner?

This usually generates debate - there are those who believe it will, especially if you adopt a Human Relations approach to the problems, and adapt the formal organization to the individual. There are others that believe politics will be an inevitable feature of the situation, however well it is designed. I use the dialectic created between these views to demonstrate the alternative analyses and solutions presented by rational and political frames of reference. To highlight this I get the class to analyze the case as one of organizational politics, and produce exaggerated scenarios of the politics that may characterize the situation described in the case.

By the time this discussion ends, we have probably used an hour to an hour and a half of class time and established a very important principle: that the same organizational situation can be understood in different ways, according to how it is framed. In other words, I have introduced the problem of analysis in a very basic way; I have also succeeded in showing them that they have a favored way of looking at organizational situations, which often tends to exclude or at least under-rate the possibility or importance of other ways of constructing the situation.

This leads me directly to the third theme of the class: that we can understand organization and management through metaphor. Given that the class has experienced the use of metaphor - since they have been shown the nature of their own favored metaphors, and learned to re-interpret the same situation in different ways they are very receptive to the idea. They have already learned the main message of the course, which subsequent weeks will refine and develop. My task in discussing this is thus an easy one. Building directly on the experience of the case, I make the following points (the main themes of chapters 1 and 10 of Images):

(a) management ideally involves a process of thinking/analyzing/acting and that by thinking and understanding in self-critical ways managers have an improved basis for action. While it is true that the pressures of managerial work often lead to a process of acting without much thought and analysis, I suggest that managers who are to act intelligently and constructively need to have a clear understanding of the situation in which they are acting. For this purpose, it is imperative that they develop ways of thinking or theorizing about the situation in which they are working. I emphasize that thinking and theorizing is an essential aspect of management and that there is nothing as practical as a good theory. I also emphasize that all practice is based on a theory of one kind or another; so it's as well to be aware of our theories. This sets the basis for the second point:

(b) I suggest to them that managers, like people in everyday life, think through images or metaphors. I introduce the idea that we can use images/metaphors as tools for thought and analysis: that we can learn to see the same situation in different ways. I typically include a discussion on the nature of metaphor here, emphasizing that any metaphor is always partial and one-sided, and unable to grasp the total nature of the situation to which it is applied (See my ASQ article "Paradigms, Metaphors and Puzzle Solving in Organization Theory", 1980, for a full discussion.) Hence the need for pluralist or multi-sided approaches to organizational analysis. (Chapters 1 and 10 of Images provide a comprehensive introduction to all of the above ideas.)

(c) I then go on to my next point: that organization is enacted image/metaphor. In other words, I introduce them to the idea that organizations become expressions of the metaphors through which managers manage. The mechanistic organization is the product of a mechanistic mode of thought. Other metaphors produce different kinds of organization.

This "enactment" of metaphor is discussed in Chapter 11 of Images, but it is too early in the course to assign the reading. I thus just hint at what is to come, taking the opportunity to introduce the basic idea.

It is only now at this late stage of the class that I discuss the detailed course outline and assignments for the course. The first half of the class will have established the basic aims and objectives of the course and given them practical experience of what the analysis of organizational situations involves, so that they appreciate the rationale and significance of what they are doing. They have given their full attention to the class discussion, without the distraction of wondering where everything fits together. They are themselves able to answer what earlier might have been raised as questions. Typically, I take them through the course outline, trying to make as many links back to earlier class discussion. I emphasize that the case study which I have designed as the class project gives them an opportunity to apply different metaphors in practice, just as we applied the ideas in a crude way to the case study discussed in the first half of class.

By the end of this first class, I have thus introduced the aims and objectives of the course, given them practical experience as to what it will involve, and set the context for the next class discussion which will focus on the mechanistic approach to understanding organizations. The remainder of the course teaches the class to see and understand organizations through different perspectives and to integrate them into a coherent method of organizational analysis.

The assigned readings from COT are designed to supplement those from Images, and to reinforce the points made in the class. The MINDSTRETCHERS (COT #1-20) provide exercises in seeing situations in different ways. They can be done at home, and time permitting, discussed in class - the choice is yours. Either way, the student is encouraged to learn the art of "reading", "framing" and "reframing". The reading "The Short and Glorious History of Organization Theory" by Charles Perrow (COT #21) is assigned to provide a general overview of the development of organization theory.

Note:

The above class plan easily fills a three hour class period. If one and a half hour periods are the norm, cover points 1 and 4 in the first class, and treat topics 2 and 3 in the second. Split topics 2 and 3 if classes are limited to 1 hour class. The plan is highly flexible.

THEME 2:   THE MACHINE METAPHOR

In teaching this theme I usually have four objectives (relevant
readings in COT are shown in brackets):

1. To explore the nature of mechanistic organization and its
links with the concepts of bureaucracy, classical management
theory and scientific management (COT #s 21, 22).

2. To illustrate successes and failures, and the
circumstances influencing its effectiveness (COT #s 24, 74,
77).

3. To illustrate the social consequences of mechanization and
the bureaucratization of society, providing the start of a
general critique that will link with Theme 9 on domination
and control, to be examined later in the course (COT #s 23,
25, 26, 75).

4. To help students appreciate the force of metaphorical
thinking by showing how the mechanistic approach to
organization has become a taken for granted mindset, and to
open the way to alternative modes of thinking.

As noted earlier, the key choice for the instructor is whether
the class is to be structured with a theoretical or practical
focus.   If theoretical, the above issues can be approached
directly, i.e. as issues.*

If teaching a course with a practical focus, I would begin with
the case A Visit to McDonalds (COT #77), using this as a platform
to discuss the McDonald's organization in more general terms.
The case is a good one to generate student discussion and
involvement early in the course, because so many students have
had direct experience of the organization. By getting beneath
the surface and showing them how the organization really works,
one can demonstrate how an understanding of the underlying
metaphor can transform one's understanding.   After this case
students will no longer see a McDonald's or other fast food
restaurant in the same way!   I use the exercise on American
Football (COT #74) for a similar purpose - within or outside
class. The exercise is excellent for getting students to see
beyond the obvious, and discover underlying principles of
organization.

---

*The same point applies in teaching the classes relating to other
themes, so I will not make this point again - those wishing to
teach theory can approach the issues identified in the class
plans "head on", selecting cases and readings to illustrate
detailed points.

As indicated in the analysis presented in the CASENOTES these cases can be used to explore mechanistic organization and scientific management in practice, and by examining the reasons underlying McDonald's success, it is possible to systematize the factors influencing the effectiveness of mechanistic-bureaucratic management. An initial formulation of these factors would include the ideas that mechanistic organization is efficient and effective when:

(a) the primary task is that of producing a simple, well understood product in a cost-efficient way:

(b) the environment is stable and/or controllable, and does not impose fluctuating demands upon the production system;

(c) there is an abundant supply of non-unionized compliant labor, easily trained and easily replaced.

The McDonald's case provides a perfect exemplar of Tayloristic control over the efficiency of labour, and an introduction to the principles of bureaucratic organization. As discussed in the CASENOTES, the case also provides an opportunity to examine how McDonald's combines a capacity for innovation (through the more organic activities of its head office), with an all-out commitment to efficiency through the mechanistic approach to organization and management that controls the process of production, beginning with suppliers and ending with service in retail outlets. The differentiation within the organization provides a valuable introduction to the principle of differentiation and integration, to be discussed in classes relating to the organismic metaphor.

The McDonald's case can be used as a platform for looking at the influence and success of the mechanistic approach to organization more generally. For example, many franchising systems use variations of the McDonald's model. So long as the work being organized can be controlled to guarantee the production of standardized products (on which the whole rationale, image and success of franchising systems depends) mechanistic principles can often be used with good effect. We find such systems of organization being introduced in many different areas of the economy, e.g. house painting, roofing, specialist automotive services (e.g. mufflers, transmissions, windscreen replacement), house cleaning, as well as in the fast food industry. By looking at the similarities between the services provided i.e. they are relatively straightforward and capable of routinization, and then looking at the circumstances under which problems are likely to arise, one can begin to systematize the conditions under which the mechanistic approach to organization encounters difficulties. These represent the "flip-side" of the factors underlying success: (a) unpredictable tasks that may involve processing uncontrollable and non-standardized inputs; (b) changing environmental circumstances, creating a need for adaptive rather than repetitive behavior; (c) employees that seek more than money and a routine job; (d) situations that are unionized, and where employees can join together to control the organizational "machine".

A discussion of these problems can then be widened to look at the weaknesses of the mechanistic approach and its unfortunate social consequences. To do this I like to start by showing the first thirteen and a half minutes of Charlie Chaplin's film Modern Times (see CASENOTES), building to a critique of how Taylorism pervades the modern workplace in many forms e.g. on the assembly-line (an excuse to discuss the contribution of Henry Ford), and in the "office factories" dominated by routine paper processing e.g. in many banks and insurance companies. The material in Images, Chapter 2, and COT (#s 21, 22, 23, 24, 25 and 26) focussing on various aspects of the mechanistic approach provide supplementary resources. For example the case illustrations provided in COT #25 "Working Under Mechanized Systems of Production," provide plenty of raw material for discussion, or as background reading, and also have relevance to the critique of domination that will be picked up under Theme 9. It is my experience that students will have an excellent stock of knowledge about the problems of mechanistic-bureaucratic organization - in government, in the factory, in the use of MBO and other highly rationalized systems of planning and control, and even in the way their current education is being shaped, so the instructor only has to mobilize this knowledge and experience, and allow them to see the problems as a product of the mechanistic mindset that produces them.

One can end the class/classes on this theme on an up note by emphasizing how the problems and weaknesses of the mechanistic approach can be overcome through the use of other metaphors. One must strive to help students see that the traps of one particular metaphor can be tacked through the strengths of others.

THEME 3: ORGANIZATIONS AS ORGANISMS

The material to be covered under this theme is very broad and wide ranging since the organismic metaphor has provided the dominant framework for the development of organization theory over the last 30 years. However, the themes which have emerged from this work are very clear, so it is a very easy area to organize at both the micro and macro level of analysis, there being considerable overlap between the two levels because they draw upon similar ideas. In a general overview course on organizational theory and analysis, I would devote at least two three-hour sessions to this metaphor, though there is enough material here for a whole course. Indeed, if you look at most courses on organization theory and design at the macro level, in organizational development, and corporate strategy, we find that they are almost totally devoted to theories considered in Chapter 3 of Images. The instructor is thus faced with a choice as to the kind of detail in which the material is to be taught. The approach which I am advocating here is appropriate to both the general overview course and in depth courses in this area. It's just a question of elaborating and developing the basic ideas through means of the ideas presented in Chapter 3 of Images and the readings and cases presented in COT.

My approach to teaching the area is to demonstrate the basic principles associated with the organismic metaphor through cases, concrete examples, and case exercises so that the student can learn to put the ideas into practice. My aim is to get them to see the power and possibilities offered by organic as opposed to mechanistic thinking, and in particular, to achieve a number of more specific objectives (relevant COT #s shown in brackets):

1. To create a detailed understanding of the distinctions between mechanistic, matrix and organic organizations and related ideas about the variety of the species (COT #27).

2. To illustrate principles of contingency theory: the idea of "good fit" (congruency) within the organization and between organization and environment; how there is no one best way of organizing - there are always strengths and weaknesses (COT #s 29, 30, 32, 49, 78, 79, 80).

3. To illustrate the principle of differentiation and integration (COT #33).

4. To illustrate the importance of strategy and choice in the process of developing "good fit" (organizations, unlike organisms do not always "adapt" spontaneously), and to introduce the debate between adaptation, selection and enactment views (COT #35, 37, 38).

5. To illustrate how environments are constantly changing and how the new forms of turbulence are encouraging the development of organic networking, within and between organizations, and new concepts of collective strategy (COT #27, 31, 34, 35, 39, 81).

6. To highlight the differences between "population ecologists" and "social ecologists" and their way of explaining the relationship between organization and environment.

My preferred mode of developing these issues is through a well developed sequence of case studies. The Paradoxical Twins case (COT #79) presents a great foundation, introducing elements of points 1 to 4 above (See CASENOTES). I follow this with Scholar

Educational Products (COT #80), and counterpose this with the case of 3M (COT #49), supplemented with a video to bring it to life (See CASENOTES on Scholar and 3M). These three cases provide a practical means of introducing many ideas about the contingency approach and the problem of dealing with environmental change. I use the scheme in COT #78, which provides a method for plotting organizational characteristics within a contingency mode to analyze the organization-environment interface in these and many other cases in COT.

I achieve my remaining teaching objectives in relation to the organismic theme raising relevant points systematically, referring to the readings in Images and COT, as referenced above. The case study on the financial services industry (COT #81) can be useful in illustrating the turbulence leading to more network forms of organization and interorganizational collaboration. Other assigned readings contain numerous examples of the problems posed to organizations in turbulent environments. Much can be done to help students by highlighting salient issues in class, but I also expect them to work on their own, drawing out the implications of the readings within the context provided by Chapter 3 of Images, and the ideas discussed in class. Their work on the course assignment i.e. their own case study, often provides a focus for them to do this.

One important point to remember at this stage of the course is that the assigned case studies e.g. on McDonald's, Scholar, 3M, will contain cultural, political and other dimensions that are not fully explored in class. However, discussion in subsequent classes will be able to return to these issues, providing the valuable lesson that all organizational characteristics are intertwined, and do not fall exclusively within one class topic or another. The instructor can play a valuable role in drawing these links.

As suggested earlier there is certainly no shortage of ideas and material in relation to this theme. The basic problem is one of focus, and deciding what is to be emphasized or glossed. These are issues that every instructor will have to decide for him or herself. The cases and readings in COT, together with Chapter 3 of Images, should be seen as springboards for getting into issues. For example, the COT item on organizational technologies (#29) and that on organizational environments (#30) only provide the most general perspective on these issues. Some instructors will want to go into these in great depth. They should supplement the basic framework that is provided with their own ideas and material through interventions/mini-lectures that put "meat on the bones." In my experience the instructor can do much to energize the class and enhance personal effectiveness in the classroom by providing this kind of highly focussed input.

THEME 4:   THE BRAIN METAPHOR

In teaching this theme I usually set five objectives (relevant COT #s shown in brackets):

1. To introduce the idea that organization is about information and information-processing (COT #s 28, 39, 44, 45).

2. To deepen the exploration initiated in Chapter 4 of Images on the questions: How can we organize to promote learning and innovation? How can we create intelligent organizations?

3. To explore the barriers to learning and innovation created in bureaucratic organizations and many management control systems (COT #s 41, 42, 82, 83, 84).

4. To explore the principles of single - and double-loop learning, and ideas about holographic organization: as a means of systematizing the principles through which managers can develop learning-oriented organizations that self-organize (COT #s 40, 43, 46, 47, 48, 49).

5. And, time permitting, to explore the links between left and right brained thinking and the dominance of left-brained organizational characteristics (COT #84).

Treatment of this metaphor can easily become very theoretical. But it can also be very practical as well. The idea that organization is really about information is vividly illustrated in the way computers are reshaping the corporate world (COT #s 39, 44, 45). The idea that conventional bureaucratic organizations systematically constrain the use of intelligence (bounded rationality), discussed in Images Chapter 4 is an extremely powerful one. An introduction along these lines provides a powerful means of introducing the idea that the brain metaphor can be used to organize for learning and intelligence in a proactive way?

I develop this theme by asking what can be learned from organizations that have an outstanding record for learning and innovation. To pursue this I go back to the 3M video shown the previous week, supplemented by the written description of the company's approach to innovation outlined in COT #49. This case allows students to see how innovative companies are driven by a commitment to innovation and change that is built into the corporate culture, and the structures and processes through which they operate on a daily basis. It is useful to recall the contrast between 3M's approach to innovation and that in the Scholar Educational case to drive the point home.

I often follow this with the video on Apple Corporation under

Steve Jobs (see CASENOTES) to illustrate an innovative company with a very different style. How do 3M and Apple differ in their approach to innovation? What can be learned from the differences? Questions such as these promote a useful line of discussion, initiating debate about the nature and significance of the two corporate cultures (Apple is youthful and fun loving, 3M is older, better established, and more adversarial), and the way, innovation has been institutionalized in the two companies. In 3M there are formal roles for idea generators, champions, sponsors and orchestrators (see COT #49). In Apple organization is much more informal. But the all-out commitment to innovation, the way corporate cultures support this, the facilitating roles of managers, and the looseness and flexibility granted innovators within the context of the total corporation are obvious in both. The strong cultural aspects of the cases provide a good basis for progression to the next course theme, and can be flagged for attention without getting into the details of how the cultures are created and sustained - an important theme for the classes on corporate culture. (The fact that more than one metaphor can be used to frame understanding of a particular case is a point that helps the student appreciate the process of organizational analysis in a particularly rich way).

These examples of successful innovative organizations provide an excellent counterpoint for considering the pathologies found in more bureaucratic organizations, the next major theme to be explored. To illustrate common barriers to learning I use the two short cases presented in COT #s 82 and 83 (see CASENOTES). To systematize these, I relate the detailed examples in the cases to three generalized principles discussed in Chapter 4 of Images: (a) bureaucratic structures fragment intelligence (bounded rationality) and create institutional barriers to learning; (b) bureaucratic accountability often serves to create defective behavior that blocks learning; and (c) hierarchical structures often generate gaps between what people say and what they do.

By examining how organizations block learning, students gain further insights on the organizational arrangements that promote innovation. They also grasp the immense problems facing so many contemporary organizations in this regard. I hammer the lessons home by referring students to the example of the Challenger disaster (see COT #41) and through an analysis of some of the dysfunctional consequences of budgeting and control systems. I use the example of how police in England systematically distorted statistics on solved crimes as an example (see COT #42). There is an enormous literature on the game playing around budgets and controls for those wishing to pursue this theme in greater depth.

Using the above cases as practical background, it is now possible to discuss concepts relating to single - and double-loop learning, and ideas about self-organization and holographic organization very effectively. Ideas about single - and double-loop learning are simple and powerful, and are well presented in Images Chapter 4 and COT #48. The case example of Japanese organization presented in COT #40 illustrates cybernetic self-regulation in practice. (The extent to which you wish to introduce students to the theory of cybernetics at this point is up to you. I think that it's important, but time may not permit adequate treatment. Chapter 4 of Images introduces central concepts, so you may feel this adequate).

On the question of self organization and the holographic principle I feel very strongly. These concepts are powerful ones, and if grasped, can provide a valuable reference point in forging organizations where bureaucratic characteristics are minimized. They offer a new way of thinking about organization that can break the bureaucratic mindset. For so many people organization means bureaucratization in one form or another. New concepts of organization are needed to break this mindset, and I believe that the holographic/self-organizing principle offers strong possibilities. I thus like to spend some time getting my class to understand the power of the holographic viewpoint.

Time permitting, I evoke the holographic imagery presented in Images Chapter 4, and try to show how my four principles of holographic organization can help managers in very practical ways. To illustrate the whole in parts principle in a general sense I use the example of Magna International (see COT #47). Magna boss Frank Stronach is driven by a political principle- "fair enterprise" - but the underlying principles are holographic. To illustrate the four crucial elements of holographic organization I emphasize the following:

Requisite Variety - an indispensible concept for building parts that contain the whole; of great use in designing product and planning teams, learning about the environment, etc.

Redundant functions - a powerful concept for creating flexibility and capacities for self organization that promote adaptation. To illustrate I use a Volvo publicity film on the use of autonomous work groups at the Kalmar plant, and the manufacturing system illustrated in COT #46.

Learning to learn - absolutely critical for designing control and decision making systems that allow for intelligent evolution. The dysfunctional consequences of the single-loop learning systems evident in the case studies referred to above (especially COT #s 42, 82, 83) provide the rationale for looking for double loop alternatives. Another opportunity to warn about the single-loop limitations of many approaches to MBO, MIS, PPBS etc.

Minimum critical specification - a way of minimizing

bureaucratic constraints and over organizing. If situations are over-organized, they can't self organize. To illustrate I recall and develop the examples presented in Chapter 4 of Images and how the principle points toward a facilitating role for managers. Managers become enablers: creating the conditions necessary for self-organization and coherent direction to emerge.

These four principles turn bureaucratic organization on its head, providing a means of creating organizations that are organized, but not in a bureaucratic sense. Many of the excellent companies discussed by Peters and Waterman in In Search of Excellence possess these holographic properties, even though they are not conceptualized and described in these terms. There is great resonance between the principles of holographic organization and much successful organizational practice. By adopting a practical focus on this very theoretical concept, it's possible to help students gain new insights about the guiding principles that can be used to shape organization in practice.

Finally, if time permits, I round off discussion on Theme 4 by focussing on another aspect of the brain metaphor: the distinction between left and right brained thinking. There is a clear relationship between the rigour, linearity and discipline of bureaucratic organization and "left-brained" thinking on the one hand, and of "right-brained" thinking and the free flowing forms of activity that spur creativity, on the other. The paradox is well illustrated in COT #84. The overall message: as we organize, we run the danger of squeezing creativity out. Nowadays, creativity is at a premium. We need to find ways of getting it back in!.

Overall, the ideas explored under Theme 4 on the brain metaphor thus provide a valuable means of opening the student's mind to the creative possibilities in tackling the process of organizing.

THEME 5:   THE CULTURE METAPHOR

In teaching this theme I usually have the following objectives (relevant COT #s shown in brackets):

1. To show how organizations are cultures, and how corporate culture is created and sustained (COT #16, 50, 51, 85, 86).

2. To show how a focus on the dynamics of culture and the methods used to create and manage meaning can open the door to new styles of management (COT #50, 51, 52, 53, 54, 55, 86, 88).

3. In the process, to illustrate different kinds of corporate culture, e.g. Apple Computer, 3M, Mary Kay Cosmetics,

Servicemaster, Tandem, and time permitting, cross cultural differences, e.g. between Japanese, British, American, Canadian organizations (COT #40, 54, 55, 56, 57, 86, 88, 89).

4. To illustrate how corporate culture can become a dominant mindset that traps and controls organizational members, often linked to political or unconscious factors (COT #86).

5. To illustrate the relationship between corporate culture and sub-culture, how they often exist in an uneasy tension (COT #87, 89, 90).

6. To examine the relationship between culture and organizational change, and the links between variations in corporate culture and subculture and the principles of differentiation and integration (COT #86, 90, 91).

7. To examine the relations between corporate culture, power, and politics, and how transformations in corporate culture often hinge on the politics of control and the "management of meaning" (COT #57, 86, 90, 91, 97, 102).

8. To point to the links between culture and ideology, as a means of highlighting some of the reinterpretations that will emerge when the class examines the psychic prison and domination metaphors later in the course.

To achieve these aims I find it useful to organize the above issues in accordance with the following broad themes, which can be revised and elaborated to suit your particular needs:

(a) The nature and significance of corporate culture

I typically begin by showing a video on Mary Kay Cosmetics (see CASENOTES): to illustrate the creation of culture as a system of reality in a rather extreme way. The advantage of this video is that the whole idea of corporate culture becomes clearly visible. The hoopla of Mary Kay cannot be missed: it is clear that we have in these organizations distinctive systems of reality that are created and sustained through many kinds of symbolic action. Against this backdrop, together with the experience of the videos on Apple Computer and 3M, shown in previous classes, it is then easy to invite students to look for aspects of culture in more mundane organizations. The focus on highly visible aspects of corporate culture allows one to develop the idea that in many organizations culture is often all but invisible (because we are too close and too much a part of it to see and understand its nature). All organizations are cultures. They all rest on the construction of a shared reality of some kind. It's just a question of learning to see and understand how the reality construction occurs. I use COT #s 16, 51 and 85 to provide frameworks through which they can do this.

The same platform can be used to move to a discussion of cross-national aspects of corporate culture if you wish (e.g. of Japanese or British organizations) to show that we are dealing with a universal phenomenon. Just as Japanese and Mary Kay type organizations may seem strange and extreme to staid Westerners, staid Western organizations are strange and extreme from other vantage points.

The aim of all this is to get students to see and understand culture and corporate culture as socially constructed reality, created and sustained through various kinds of values, norms, rituals, beliefs, language, ideology, etc.. COT #s 16, 40, 50, 51, 52, 54, 55, and 85 are particularly relevant. Focus on the ones that will help you organize a presentation that will suit your particular needs.

(b) Corporate culture and the management of meaning.

Against this background it is easy to see that the management of meaning is central to the managerial process generally, and that skilled leaders, opinion shapers and those who exert a formative influence on corporate culture are skillful in this unsung art. I move now to take a closer look at how culture hinges on shared meaning, and how managers and others shape the system of meaning within their organization. To do this, one can "zero-in" on the details of the cases and readings referred to above. How does a shared culture emerge in Mary Kay, 3M, Apple Computer, Tandem Corporation? Take a closer look at Steve Jobs' managerial style at Apple, or at the examples presented in COT #s 52, 53, 54, 55, 86, 87, 88. Use COT exercise #85 as a framework for organizing one's thoughts, and conducting a detailed analysis. Get students to apply the ideas to organizations that they know. The aim should be to get them to be able to analyze and understand how corporate culture is created, in a very practical way.

(c) Corporate culture as a mindset, and potential trap.

A cohesive corporate culture can provide a basis for success, but it can also serve as a trap. I use the Perfection or Bust case (COT #86) to develop this theme, and to illustrate how a recipe for success can turn into a constraining mindset that prevents one from achieving key tasks effectively. Many organizations suffer the fate of the small company described in this case. It is also useful here to draw links in relation to the way Steve Jobs had a strong personal, and at times idiosyncratic, vision for

Apple products that from a business success standpoint
created many problems, linked to his eventual departure from
the organization (see cot #57). The team that produced the
Macintosh computer was led in Jobs' phrase "by a monomaniac
with a vision", achieving spectacular results, but at the
expense of certain blindspots. An exploration of these
ideas helps to warn students of the two-edged nature of
culture, and possible downside effects, setting links to
the political and psychic prison metaphors to be examined
later.

(d) Culture and counter-culture: competing definitions of
reality? Part of a struggle for control of corporate
reality? Corporate culture can create problems in relation
to the process of organizational change.

Corporate culture is sometimes uniform and cohesive, but
more often it is not. As an illustration I build around the
Fortress Insurance case (COT #90). It provides an excellent
illustration of clashes between culture and sub-culture, and
raises important issues in relation to the political aspects
of corporate culture and problems of organizational change,
and with regard to the principle of differentiation and
integration (discussed in relation to the organismic
metaphor), in that it is often necessary to preserve
differences within a pattern of corporate culture, while
binding the whole together. (The discussion can throw fresh
light on the Scholar Educational Products case considered in
an earlier class). The political significance of culture
clashes, and the power aspects of the management of meaning
begin to become evident in discussing Fortress, and can be
further explored through COT #s 87, 97, and 102. These
three cases - Maria Theresa, Sunnyvale Youth Centre and
Quality Coop - all speak to the theme of culture and counter
culture, with strong links to the politics of organization.
The links between corporate culture, politics and
organizational change are also brought out in the Rainbow
Financial Services case (COT #91). Culture can be a real
block to change - a mindset that traps an organization
within an unsatisfactory mode of operation.

(e) Culture, politics, ideology and control.

The political significance of culture clashes, becomes very
evident from the Fortress Insurance case, which provides an
excellent springboard to integrate the political and
cultural metaphors with regard to issues such as the
management of meaning, dominant ideology, and the process of
control. The Sunnyvale Youth Centre case (COT #97) provides
another excellent illustration of the dynamics of culture
and counter-culture, and how meaning can be systematically
managed for political ends. Sink or Swim: Reflections on a

Corporate Training Program (COT #88) is also useful for illustrating the power dimension underlying the construction of organizational meaning systems. They provide excellent points of transition from cultural to political metaphors.

THEME 6:   THE POLITICAL METAPHOR

My objectives in teaching this theme are usually as follows (relevant COT #s shown in brackets):

1.   To illustrate the political dimensions of organizations: how organizations are political systems (COT #s 57, 58, 63, 92, 93, 94, 97, 98).

2.   To develop concrete skills in the political analysis of organizations, using the interests, conflict, power model presented in chapter 6 of Images (COT #s 92, 93, 97, 98, 99, 100, 101, 102, 103, 104, 105, 106, 107, 108, 110).

3. To provide a detailed understanding of the nature and use of power in organizations (COT #s 64, 97, 99, 100, 101, 103, 104, 105, 106, 107, 108, 110).

4. To provide an introduction to the skills of political management and conflict resolution in pluralist organizations (COT #s 59, 60, 61, 62, 95, 96).

5. To illustrate that organizations are rationalizing rather than rational, and how rationality is best understood through a concept of political rationality (COT #63).

6. To examine organizations through the lens of comparative government: as unitary, pluralist or radical systems, or in terms of the "forms of rule" illustrated in Exhibit 6.1 of Images (page 145).

7. To raise the issue of gender and gender-related politics (COT #s 65, 100).

There is an enormous amount that can be taught in relation to this theme. I teach these ideas in abbreviated form in my general overview course on organizational analysis, and in much more depth in a full course on Organizational Politics, Power & Conflict. The problem facing most instructors will be to decide what can be reasonably covered in the time available. The following approach may help you to decide.

My aim from the beginning is to show students how they can analyze organizational politics in a practical way, using the interests, conflict, power model presented in Chapter 6 of

Images. To cut to the core of the issues I like to begin with a role-play (Global Inc., COT #93), which is designed to illustrate the political dynamics found in many organizations. This simulates a meeting shaped by hidden agendas, conflicting interests, coalition building and power-plays (see CASENOTES). The roleplay serves to bring corporate politics to life in the classroom and give students first hand experience of "reading" organizational situations from a political standpoint.

These skills can be further developed by building on a variety of case studies. COT #92 The University as a Political System provides a means of conducting an analysis of the structure of interests, conflict and sources of power in a university - an exercise that can be done outside class if you wish. COT #s 104 (The Lakeside Literary Magazine) and COT #105 (The Upstage Theatre Company) provide excellent introductory cases that can be used as a follow up to the above exercises. All these materials help to build on the initial insights emerging from the Apple Computer, Fortress Insurance and Sunnyvale Youth Centre cases considered in classes relating to the culture metaphor. Together with Conflict at Riverside (COT #98), Quality Coop (COT #102), Problems in the Machine Shop (COT #107), and the case study of the auto industry in Final Offer (COT #110), they illustrate political problems in a cross section of different organizations, though you may wish to delay use of Final Offer until the classes on the domination metaphor.

There are a number of cases and exercises that are especially useful for examining power relations within an organization- see for example COT #s 99 (The Handgrenade), 100 (Jersey Packers), 101 (Information Services), 103 (Dillworth Extension) and 106 (Tipdale Engineering). Read the CASENOTES on these and see which are best suited to your purposes. The analysis of power presented on pages 158-185 of Images provides a systematic framework against which this can be done.

The case on Mary Cunningham (COT #65), and Jersey Packers (COT #100 provide good starting points for discussing gender relations. As will be apparent from the material in Images Chapters 6 and 7 there is an enormous amount that can be covered here, especially by considering organizations from the standpoint of male and female archetypes and the role of patriarchy (See Images pages 178-183, 210-212).

After showing how to analyze political aspects of organization in general terms with a focus on the analysis of interests, power, and coalition building (the essential themes illustrated in the above), I am now ready to approach the issue of political management, with a special focus on how to understand and approach conflict. By now students will be well aware that organizations are rationalizing rather than rational, that conflict is inevitable, and that the managerial task hinges on how it is to be managed. The readings and exercises in COT #s 58, 59, 60, 61, 62, 63, 94,95, 96 all address this issue in one way or another and can be used to develop understanding of the problems of conflict management. The reading and analytical schemes presented in Images, pages 185-194 are also very relevant here. Select the readings and cases that will help you achieve your specific aims.

Against this background it is now easy and useful to look at organizational politics from a broad analytical perspective that will be relevant in making a transition to the domination metaphor later in the course. I like to draw the distinction between unitary, pluralist and radical perspectives, and to invite students to use this schema for thinking about the relations between organizations and society, and for understanding the kind of organization with which one is dealing. Pluralist ideas and strategies do not work in radicalized organizations! I also like to draw links with the typology of forms of rule presented on page 145 of Images, to emphasize the inherently political nature of organizations and provide a further link to the societal perspective to be considered under the domination theme.

My plan for teaching the political metaphor thus begins with a focus on the practical problems of understanding and managing conflict, and moves from this to a measure of social critique, a theme that will receive full expression in examining the domination metaphor, and to an extent, in the psychic prison metaphor as well.

THEME 7: THE PSYCHIC PRISON METAPHOR

In teaching this theme I usually set the following objectives (relevant COT #s shown in brackets):

   1. To focus attention on the idea that organizations and their members can get "trapped" by the realities they create (COT #s 11, 12, 13, 14, 17, 18, 37, 66, 67, 86).

   2. To explore some behavioral reasons why this occurs (COT #s 10, 11, 12, 13, 14, 17, 18, 66, 67, 84, 86, 88).

   3. To explore psychoanalytic and other explanations associated with the unconscious (COT #s 66, 67, 68, 69, 86).

   4. To explore the ideological aspects of entrapment, and the links between the ideologies that underpin modern organizations and those underpinning modern society/societies (COT #s 56, 69, 88, 89, 102).

5. To show how the exploitative and domineering aspects of all the above processes link to the domination theme to be explored later in the course.

Consideration of these issues flows very naturally from material covered in relation to the cultural and political metaphors. The former introduces the idea that organizations and their members can get trapped by aspects of corporate culture. The political metaphor introduces the role of power. Putting the two together we enter the arena of ideological power plays, conscious and unconscious, taking us right into issues associated with the psychic prison metaphor.

My approach in introducing the issues is to refer to the modes of entrapment illustrated in cases considered earlier in the course. For example, Perfection or Bust (COT 90) and to an extent the Fortress Insurance case (COT 90) illustrate how organizations can become trapped by culture, and the politics that sustain belief systems. The Scholar Educational Products case (COT 80) illustrated how organizational belief systems get in the way of successful adaptation to a changing environment. Quality Coop (COT 102) has a dimension of ideological struggle linking to competing social values in society at large. Sink or Swim (COT 88) illustrated the development of commitment to organizational values through ideological processes with conscious and unconscious dimensions. So there are many ways of introducing the themes to be explored more directly in relation to the psychic prison metaphor.

In teaching the metaphor there is a great opportunity to introduce a measure of critical reflection on how organizations operate in practice, and indeed a full blown social critique, taking one right into the theme of domination. Instructors will always face a choice as to how far they go in this. The critique can be limited to the idea that the metaphor shows a way of creating a more reflective approach to management that will help one escape from undesirable traps - a solidly managerial approach. Or one can go with a more fully developed "radical humanist" critique of organization and management generally. One also faces the choice in this of how theoretical one wants to be: treating the problem of entrapment as no more than a practical issue (i.e. the metaphor can help improve managerial practice), with the risk that one creates ways of strengthening the mode of entrapment at a societal level by helping managers strengthen the ideological bonds, versus the full blown radical humanist view developed by Burrell and Morgan in Sociological Paradigms and Organizational Analysis (Heinemann, 1979), confronting very directly the view that organization hinges on ideological domination that is systemic, and deeply political. Even in practical courses I try to push as far as I can towards the latter, since I believe that most students of management are in dire need of education about the ideological dimension of the role they play as managers. The issue provides a springboard linking to the ethical dimensions of organization and management to be explored more fully in relation to the domination metaphor.

Here are some ideas on how one can achieve the objectives referred to above.

1. Approach the issue of how people and organizations become trapped by the realities they create by making reference to earlier cases, using the introduction described above. Make particular use of Perfection or Bust (COT 86), and develop links with the examples and ideas presented in Images, pages 109-203. There is an opportunity to return to the issue of the social construction/enactment of reality, discussed in Images, Chapter 6, and the problem of human alienation.

2. The behavioral factors underlying entrapment can be explored by focussing on the issue of framing and reframing illustrated in many of the exercises in the Mindstretchers section of COT, emphasizing how perception is culturally learned, and how it always creates biases and blindspots. There is an opportunity here to return to discuss ideas on the enactment of organizational reality and understanding of the wider environment (COT 37). The thrust of the framing and reframing idea can be to show ways of escaping from traps and one sided ways of seeing, an important objective of Images, and the approach to organizational analysis that I have tried to develop throughout most of my work. Another important behavioral explanation of entrapment is found in many group and other socialization processes that breed conformity. The concept of "groupthink" (COT 67) provides an obvious way of illustrating this idea. Sink or Swim (COT 88) may be used as a case focussing on the way organizations try to socialize people into accepting a corporate ethos and mindset.

3. The psychoanalytic and deep unconscious reasons through which individuals construct personal, interpersonal, organizational and societal realities is a major issue that can be explored in enormous depth if one is inclined, using Freudian, Jungian and other perspectives. The material in Images Chapter 7 and related bibliographical notes points in many directions. Specific case studies are presented in COT #s 66, 68, 69. (The combined possibilities here are such that there is no option other than to choose your particular path and desired emphasis). My favored approach is to use a video case called Discovery Toys (see CASENOTES) to create a "live" example in class that allows one to springboard to more general issues relating to unconscious gameplaying and entrapment, workaholism, compulsiveness, preoccupation with control, the psychoanalytic significance of bureaucracy, etc. etc.. Wonderful insights can emerge in relation to the hidden

basis and rationale of many personal and interpersonal aspects of organizational life. The discussion can be very specific and practical, yet at the same time draw out major theoretical insights.

4. On the ideological aspects of organization and society try building from observations about the exploitative and alienating aspects of organizational practice. For example use COT 56 as a starting point for looking at how Japanese values relating to conformity can have an alienating aspect. Use COT 69 on workaholism as a way of launching a discussion about the alienating aspects of Western ways of life, or draw out the implications of COT 88 Sink or Swim on the ideological aspects of training, the values associated with being a winner, a member of an elite group, etc.. Link all this to the argument that organizations and society are part of a common ideological superstructure - a point that I refer to in a section on page 366 of Images, but which I was unable to develop. The point about the discussion is that it should ground an understanding of organizational life in the processes that sustain society more generally. The discussion leads to important theoretical insights, and the whole rationale of the radical humanist critique of society. But it also has practical implications as well, in relation to general values and individual and corporate ethics. There are important lessons for many students here, if only in showing that they may be propagating exploitative values, or in more polemical Marxian terminology, may be lackeys of the ruling class of the society to which they belong. Organization, management, rationality etc., are inherently ideological.

5. The links to the domination metaphor flow naturally from the above, and require no additional explanation.

THEME 8: THE FLUX AND TRANSFORMATION METAPHOR

In addressing this theme I set the following objectives (relevant COT #s shown in brackets):

1. To help students appreciate that there are always deep "structural" explanations of organizational life, and that a full understanding requires an ability to look beyond surface appearances. To really understand what is shaping events in the here and now, they need an appreciation of the historical processes through which life seems to be unfolding (COT #s 19, 35, 70, 71).

2. To examine different perspectives through which such understanding can be obtained, and to appreciate that some of the major debates about the nature of organization and

society hinge on different views of the fundamental "logic"
of change.

3. To highlight the policy issues that can arise from this
kind of understanding, especially at a governmental level
(COT # 35, 70, 71).

4. To illustrate that organizations are always in flux, and
that a conceptualization of organizations as flowing "energy
fields" can provide an interesting perspective on problems of
organizational change and development.

This is probably the most difficult and challenging metaphor
discussed in Images, and the one that is the most difficult to
integrate into courses with a practical focus. Yet the policy
implications are enormous, for the metaphor identifies and
addresses some of the major societal problems being faced today.

I find that if I am teaching practical courses, e.g. to MBAs, it
is best to link some of the main issues relating to objectives 1,
2 and 3 to other metaphors, rather than address them in their own
right. For example, I sometimes link some of the implications of
autopoiesis (Images, pages 235-247) to a discussion of enactment
and the making of reality in dealing with organismic and cultural
metaphors. I link the insights on mutual causality, thinking in
"loops rather than lines", and the implications for collaborative
strategy (Images, pages 247-255) to a discussion of cybernetics
under the brain metaphor. And I link ideas about unfolding
contradictions (Images, pages 255-267) to the domination
metaphor. The arrangement is unsatisfactory, but the problems of
student motivation and the difficulties in covering all metaphors
in a single course often win the day. In this event I would
assign Chapter 8 of Images towards the end of the course, along
with Chapter 9 in discussing the domination metaphor, or split it
up in the manner suggested above. I would attempt to squeeze in
key insights as I go along, rather than teach them in a formal
manner, focussing on the key message that societally, we
desperately need to understand the "logic" that is driving the
modern world. The rhyme "There was an old lady who swallowed a
fly" (COT 19) communicates the essential message. A focus on
ethical issues in considering the domination metaphor allows one
to address some of these challenging social issues very
constructively. COT #s 35, 70 and 71 can be used to create a
practical focus for some of this discussion.

In teaching a more theoretical course, or an advanced seminar
that is going to address some of the more difficult and
challenging issues the above problems don't arise. My approach
is to work through Chapter 8 section by section, addressing the
three different logics of change in turn. I highlight the
important implications of each of the three theoretical
perspectives. Autopoiesis creates important insights about

organizational narcissism and the importance of reflecting on one's identify as a means of understanding how one sees and understands the wider world. The "loops not lines" idea provides an important methodology for understanding the dynamics of change, provides a fundamental epistemology, and shows the importance of developing systemic/collaborative strategies at an interorganizational level. The dialectical perspective highlights the major contradictions facing society today. The issues are very powerful, and could well command attention for a complete course.

The issues relating to objective 4 are somewhat easier to tackle, and are receiving increasing attention from organization development people who have been influenced by the transformational perspective articulated by Marilyn Ferguson (The Aquarian Conspiracy, Tarcher, 1980), and others who focus on the process of change in terms of quantum shifts, e.g. of consciouness, "critical mass", etc.. The perspective creates an interesting focus on the role of the manager/organizational consultant as someone whose interventions influence the nature and direction of the energy fields shaping organizational life. Follow up the ideas of Prigogine and Shelbrake, discussed on pages 371-372 of Images if you wish to develop this perspective.

THEME 9: THE DOMINATION METAPHOR

I usually teach this topic immediately after the political or psychic prison metaphors, since there is a natural progression to the theme of domination. The flux and transformation metaphor is a little more theoretical than others, and in courses with a practical focus, can get in the way of the momentum you have managed to develop. There are many practical insights associated with Theme 8 but they require more conceptual work to get at them.

In teaching the domination metaphor I usually set the following objectives (relevant COT numbers shown in brackets):

1. To place the issue of exploitation and domination in the corporate world - the seamy side of rationality - firmly in view (COT #s 56, 69, 72, 73, 88).

2. To use this as a springboard for exploring the issue of social responsibility and corporate ethics more generally, and whether the corporate world is intrinsically exploitative (COT #s 69, 73 and 109)

3. To investigate the nature of "radicalized organizations" (COT #s 98, 110).

4. To examine the source of this radicalization and of the

"us" versus "them" attitudes found in many aspects of labour/management relations, and the fundamental conflicts of interest that often shape ongoing struggles for control (COT #s 23, 25, 26, 75, 107, 110).

5. To identify some of the consequences of these ideas for the management of organizations generally, and the future of labour/management relations.

I usually begin my classes on the domination metaphor by using the video-case It's Not Working (see CASENOTES) as a platform for illustrating fundamental conflicts of interest between labour and capital. The video focuses on the closure of the U.S. Steel plant in Youngstown, Ohio in the late 1970's. The company is the town's main employer, and the community is looking at the grim prospect of high unemployment and long term decline. The video features speeches and commentaries by radicalized workers that feel "big business" is exploiting them. It provides a vivid illustration of Arthur Miller's metaphor of the discarded "orange peel": the steel company has sucked the community dry and is now throwing what's left away.

The video provides a highly evocative introduction to the idea that corporations are ultimately self serving, and can run roughshod over anyone and anything that lies in their way. It provides a clear illustration of how the logic of profitability and the "rationality" of much organizational decision making is politically based. I use the case as a platform for addressing fundamental conflicts of interest between labour and capital and the roots of the antagonistic labour management relations that have dominated industrial life for most of this century. I use it as a specific means of illustrating the nature of a radicalized organization, and in management courses, to help get students obtain a better appreciation of labour's point of view.

There are numerous ways in which the class can develop from here (using the material presented in Images Chapter 9 and COT as further points of reference):

- To focus on more detailed aspects of the nature of, and reasons for, "radicalized organizations" where open struggles for control are the norm. Use Final Offer (COT #110) which features union negotiations in the auto industry as another video case (see CASENOTES). Use Conflict at Riverside (COT #98) as a means of exploring fundamental conflicts of interest in relation to demands for "progress" and job redesign. Develop an appreciation for the differences between unitary, pluralist and radical frames of reference, as discussed in Chapter 6 of Images, and the organizational realities to which they give rise, and/or reflect. Use the case Problems in the Machine Shop (COT #107) as a way of getting into the problems of managing in a radicalized context.

- To explore other aspects of the conflict between labour and management. The existence of radicalized organizations invites an explanation. Very often this rests on a search for "villains" - unreasonable, greedy unions, or selfish, capitalistic management. My approach is to investigate the roots of conflict in a Marxian interpretation of the history of modern organization (see the discussion of this in Chapter 8 of Images). This draws attention to the logic underpinning industrial development, and gives new ways of thinking about the confrontation between labor and management, and the problems which this raises. We come to see how contradictions of interest are built into the system, and are not just attitudinal. This kind of analysis links into societal issues relating to the deskilling of work, the relationship between primary and secondary labour markets, the development of an "underclass" within developed nations and in the Third world, and why management can be seen as part of a wider process of exploitation and control. There is an enormous amount of material that can be developed here. Use Images chapters 8 and 9 as a springboard, along with COT #s 23, 25, 26, 56, 73, 75, and 107.

- To explore other aspects of exploitation e.g. in relation to occupational accidents and disease, the role of multinationals in the world economy, exploitation of the Third World, etc.. Use the material presented in Images Chapter 9 and COT #s 56 and 71 as resources.

- To explore the ethical implications of all the above. Is organization ultimately a question of values? Does it hinge on a systemic process of exploitation? Can morality provide the basis for a new stage of evolution that takes us beyond fundamental struggle and conflict? Should organizations be managed in the joint interests of all "stakeholders"? The domination metaphor primes the class for discussion of the values underpinning contemporary organizations and whether they need to be challenged and changed. This theme can be explored in numerous ways according to inclination and interest. Needless to say, the discussion is always lively! COT #107 provides one way of structuring an approach to these issues.

THEME 10: THE ART OF ORGANIZATIONAL ANALYSIS

This is my wrap-up theme, and embraces the basic aim of the course. In theory it should not be necessary, for if the classes and case assignment have done their job, students are now able to "read" the dynamics of their organization fairly well. The major project on which they are working throughout the course is

crucial here!   I   assign chapters 10 and 11 of Images in
connection with the wrap up class and reemphasize the basic
points, introducing the concept of "imaginization" as a means of
communicating the   idea that   organization is ultimately a
creative process with numerous possibilities.   The course has
focussed on the problem of "reading" organizations. The concept
of imaginization opens the way to new ways of designing and
managing them. A starting point for another course!!

IV. CASENOTES: TEACHING NOTES ON CASES AND EXERCISES

PREAMBLE

The notes on the following pages present some ideas on how the cases and exercises presented in Parts I and III of COT can be used to promote the objectives discussed in the previous section of this manual. The items follow the sequence of COT, and are supplemented by three additional video cases titled "Mary Kay", "Discovery Toys" and "It's Not Working", referred to in the class plans presented in the previous section of this manual. Obviously, constraints on the length of the manual prevent an exhaustive discussion of every case and exercise. I have thus tried to strike a happy balance by addressing the major points and issues that are raised, and when possible, to indicate some of the tactics that can be used to produce lively class discussions.

Before we get into the details, there are a number of points that I would make about the philosophy that underpins my use of cases, since these have been influential in shaping the kind of case that I have chosen to include in COT.

First, I see cases as vehicles for introducing a practical focus that can then be used to make more general theoretical points. They serve as platforms for getting to fundamental issues. Cases have a generic quality, in that they stand as exemplars of situations that may recur in different guises. I use them to help students see and recognize patterns that recur time and again.

For this purpose I like to use cases that are relatively short and easy to read. I like to emphasize that though we may be examining a humble organization like the Sunnyvale Youth Centre discussed in COT #97, the case could equally well be referring to a situation occurring in a multinational. This is not to say that a youth centre is exactly like a multinational. Rather, the point is that when you bring people together, discernable patterns of behavior often emerge. I don't use cases as statements of empirical reality e.g. about the nature of youth centres, so much as vehicles for thinking that will exercise and stretch the way we tend to see and understand organizations more generally. While the conclusions to be drawn from a particular case may be quite specific, the learning can be very general in application.

In line with these ideas, I encourage a flexible approach to the way cases are to be used. Use them as vehicles to achieve your teaching aims, bringing in whatever supplementary material you feel appropriate. Use the insights offered by a particular case to highlight or drive home a point made in the readings, or as exemplars of the points that you make in your lectures. Use them as exercises outside class, or as focal points in class. Use them to illustrate theoretical points, or as practical exercises that "zero-in" on problems and solutions. The choice is yours.

I offer the following notes in the spirit of sharing some ideas and interpretations that I find useful, rather than in terms of providing the definitive account of how the cases and exercises should be handled. Needless to say, if you have any ideas or angles that you would like to share, I will be delighted to hear of them.

MINDSTRETCHERS (COT #s 1-20)

These exercises can be done outside class. Their aim is to set an appropriate frame of reference for the course by getting students to think out of their usual mould. You can address some of the exercises in class if you wish, to create a measure of sharing and exchange of views. Try extending the range of the exercises. For example, Adrian McLean, who gave me the idea for COT #2 likes to bring an unusual object into class e.g. a travel poster or print, and then invite students to explain what it really is. Needless to say, explanations become really inventive. What a nice practical way to introduce ideas about different ways of seeing, and to launch the idea that our understanding of organizations can be equally creative.

AMERICAN FOOTBALL: A CASE OF MECHANISTIC ORGANIZATION? (COT # 74)

This exercise provides a very useful way of generating class involvement on a topic close to many students' outside interests, and for showing how principles of organization are evident in many aspects of social life.

American football provides a splendid illustration of the principles of classical management theory and scientific management in practice: for the game rests on a high degree of precision organization, coupled with various styles of authoritarian management.

Be sure to get the class to draw out the detailed links with the 5 principles of Scientific Management discussed in Chapter 2 of Images (also illustrated in the CASENOTES on A Visit to McDonalds in this manual). Every principle is clearly evident, and often very rigidly applied.

This analysis can then be used to produce a useful contrast with the games of soccer or rugby. Though these are often organized to conform with pre-arranged game plans, and are often set within an authoritarian system of management, the games themselves are much more fluid and free flowing. Play is continuous and rests on the creative interpretation and actions of the players. American football is much more mechanized, punctuated by organized halts and time-outs that allow the detailed intervention and control by management (in the form of coach and aides) on the side-lines, and high in the stands (through two-way radio, etc.). The contrasts between the games are striking, and provide perfect illustrations of mechanistic and more free-flowing modes of organization.

CHARLIE CHAPLIN'S MODERN TIMES (COT #75)

This entertaining movie (available in most university film libraries) provides excellent material for illustrating aspects of the machine and domination metaphors. It symbolizes the dehumanization that can occur when the principles of mechanistic organization are taken to an extreme. I use the first thirteen and a half minutes (to the end of the factory sequence). It is always a popular item and makes a number of very important points.

Try asking: What are the important issues raised? What are the main messages that the movie is trying to convey?

Three major responses usually emerge from discussion:

(a) It shows that the mechanization of organizations does not always work, because people are humans not machine parts; the movie illustrates the need for an approach to organization that combines human and technical requirements.

(b) It provides a humorous critique of Taylorism, illustrating how organizations can exploit and dehumanize their employees.

(c) It illustrates the mindset that shaped organizations during the first half of the twentieth century, and how the preoccupation with efficiency and control shaped an adversarial relationship between labour and management.

Each of these themes can be explored in depth. The movie is rich in evocative material that supports and refines these fundamental points. The movie provided an early warning about what would happen in large assembly-line plants. Charlie Chaplin loses his mind under the dehumanizing influence of the assembly line, providing a symbol of the alienation that would later affect many assembly-line employees.

In modern organizations employees have found ways of dealing
with and beating the system. The modern Charlie Chaplin is found
in the alienated assembly line worker, who rather than being
beaten by the system preserves his/her self-respect by getting
back at the system, e.g. through the union, or by hiding a coke
bottle in the engine of a car where it will shake loose in 3
months time; by adding a personal identification mark in the form
of a dent, nick or other imperfection. (Compare the readings in
COT #25).

EAGLE SMELTING (COT #76)

This is a wonderful case for illustrating the process of
organizational analysis, and how the same situation can be read
in many different ways. The case has many potential
interpretations or "readings," each of which gives rise to a
different way of dealing with problems at the Eagle Smelting
plant.

The line of analysis to be developed in class will depend on the
specific learning that the instructor wishes to achieve. I use it
as a general case - almost always as the first in my course: (a)
to illustrate the process of "reading" organization; (b) to show
how different readings suggest different managerial actions and
problem solutions, and (c) how the process of management and
organizational practice always implies a relationship between
theory (an explicit or implicit reading or set of assumptions)
and practice (the actions one favors). The case is ideal for
illustrating how practice is always guided by theory, and how it
is important to be aware of the theories shaping our action.

Analysis

Specific ideas on how the case discussion can be organized to
bring out these ideas are presented earlier in this manual in the
teaching notes relating to Theme I. Here I will discuss the
analysis of the case in more general terms, to illustrate its
richness, and the range of interpretations that are possible.

1. Poor communications. This is a popular interpretation that
almost always figures in student analyses. Shaped by
assumptions that Eagle Smelting is a bureaucratic
organization functioning inefficiently, various problems are
highlighted e.g. violation of the chain of command, poor
information exchange, overlapping job responsibilities,
sloppy adherence to prescribed roles. The solutions to the
perceived problems are thus bureaucratic ones, i.e. "tighten
up" the organization in all these respects.

2. Poor planning. The failure and problems are subscribed
to the machine breakdown, and the lack of an effective

stock of spare parts or set of contingency plans. Here
again the solutions become highly technical ones: better
machinery, more spare parts, emergency procedures, etc..

3. The dysfunctions of authoritarian management. Macrae is a
highly authoritarian manager; Holt also likes to give
instructions. No one asks questions. No evidence of
participation. Curtis can be seen as conditioned into a "do
as you are told" mentality. This view leads towards some kind
of human relations solution involving more participation, a
"flatter" less hierarchical form of organization, a better
match between individual and organizational needs, or some
form of contingency approach that emphasizes the importance of
matching task, structure, and people to create "good fit."

4. The plant manager is still doing his old job. Macrae is
acting as the area engineer. He wants Holt to do the job
exactly as he used to do it. He has interfered with his
colleague's responsibilities. He is unable to perform the
plant manager's role. He has interpreted "managing by walking
about" as an interfering "hands in" style of management. This
interpretation sees the problem resting with MacRae. He needs
to change his managerial style, or be replaced by someone who
can do the job.

5. "Awkward" or clashing personalities. Relations between
Macrae and Holt are frequently hot and emotional. Tempers are
quick. Curtis seems to be seething with resentment about a
missed promotion. Many managers would say he has "an attitude
problem."

Others might say he is alienated and fed up with his work, or
dislikes authority. This kind of interpretation may lead back
to some kind of human relations solution calling for more
participation and better communications, or to some kind of
fire and hire solution.

6. A search for villains. Who's to blame? This is a
frequent question guiding student analyses and leads them to
prescribe various solutions that involve firing key
offenders. In my experience the class that follows this line
of inquiry usually ends up making a case against almost
everyone. Macrae is blamed for his meddling. Holt is blamed
for not staying on top of the job. Curtis is blamed for
deliberately wrecking the job. And even Smith is sometimes
"fingered" for spending so much time away from the machine
shop.

7. Organizational politics? Are Macrae and Holt in
competition with each other? Does Holt have an eye on
MacRae's job? Does Macrae feel insecure and threatened by his
younger colleague who seems to do things in such a different

way. Do they have personal dislikes and quarrels? Are their
wives arch enemies and rivals in the local community? Does
this have an adverse influence on the work relations between
the two managers? Is Curtis truly seething with resentment
about the missed promotion? Is he looking for a way to get
revenge? Has he deliberately engineered Holt's dismissal in
the sense that he has been waiting for an opportunity to use
the conflict between Macrae and Holt for his own ends? Has he
been biding his time waiting for the perfect opportunity to
make his move? Is there informal collusion between Macrae and
Curtis? Perhaps each knows that the other dislikes Holt. Is
Macrae giving Curtis the chance to set him up? Are Smith and
Curtis in collusion? Are their actions part of a pre-conceived
plan to move against Holt and Macrae; disgruntled workers
against making a protest against incompetent management? Was
Hardy involved in the plot? Was the locomotive sabotaged? Some
of these questions may seem farfetched. The case is ambiguous
and does not speak to these points in a specific way. But all
identify possible situations. The case only presents a
fragment of the total situation; and there may well be
important details that are left out. (Note that cases <u>always</u>
present partial views of a situation, just as any given
organizational actor (whether manager or subordinate) usually
only gains a partial interpretation of the situation in which
he or she is working. Managers, like organizational analysts
have to deal with fragments, and they must realize that the
really important information may not be available. Politics,
in particular, often resides in the hidden and unstated realm
of organization, which like our case, gives primary attention
to the manifest rather than hidden facts of the case). This
line of questioning leads to a <u>political</u> interpretation of the
case, and favors solutions involving political solutions that
take into account competing interests and power relations.
The specific conflict is seen as symptomatic of deeper
political problems that need to be understood and managed
along the lines discussed in Chapter 6 of <u>Images.</u>

8. <u>A fragmented corporate culture?</u> There appears to be few
shared norms and values. Should those responsible for
managing the organization attempt to develop an overarching
system of shared meaning that would bind the organization
together in a meaningful way? This interpretation of the
situation directs attention to solutions involving <u>the
management of meaning.</u>

9. <u>A radicalized organization?</u> Are there deep divisions
between management and workers? Even though there is no
mention of a militant union, perhaps relations are
antagonistic and conflictual. Are there divisions between the
professional outsiders (Macrae and Holt) and the local
workforce? Is this a case reflecting the distinction between
"cosmopolitans" and "locals" drawn by Alvin Gouldner in his

book Patterns of Industrial Bureaucracy and Wildcat Strike? Are there important cultural differences between management and workers? Such interpretations would lead to solutions that see the episode in this case as symptomatic of a much deeper historical socio-economic problem, and lead to strategies that attempt to bridge the gulf in the same way.

The above line of questioning is by no means exhaustive. But it does serve to illustrate the complexity and potentially paradoxical nature of what seems at first sight to be a relatively straight-forward situation (the paradox rests in the fact that many of the above interpretations - which are all partial - may be simultaneously correct; they may all be combined in the nature of the situation). The task of the organizational analyst is to unravel this complexity in the best way he or she can. It involves an awareness of the fact that we typically read and understand situations in partial ways; that a comprehensive understanding requires that we ask many different questions and be aware of the framing and reframing process evident in the line of questioning posed above. We see the way our reading or theory suggests a form of practice, and how we can grasp a firm and reflective understanding between theory and practice.

Good managers and organizational analysts often develop the knack of reading situations intuitively. Some talk about gaining "a feel" for a situation, or "grabbing it with their guts," or trying to "smell" its key dimensions. In each case the process involves an interpretive process that implicitly attempts to understand the essence of the situation at hand. The process of reading developed in Images can be used to do exactly the same. By being open to the multiple interpretations of any given situation we create alternative models for understanding, alternative patterns of explanation and set the basis for alternative modes of action, problem formulation, and problem solution. We provide the basis for a mode of reflective management or organizational analysis that allows us to refine our interpretive skills, and provide a basis for the kind of insight and innovation that may allow us to transform organizations in fundamental ways.

I use the Eagle Smelting case to illustrate these basic ideas. Students, that are taken through the experience of this case should be asked to read Chapters I and 10 of Images to consolidate their learning.

A VISIT TO MCDONALD'S (COT #77)

This is an excellent case for illustrating the successful use of mechanistic organization and the principles of scientific management: McDonald's epitomizes how mechanical principles can be used to produce a standard product, at a low cost, for a mass market. The case seeks to re-create the experience of working in a McDonald's restaurant, in a way that will allow students to see the basic principles through which its retail outlets are organized on a day to day basis. The case illustrates how predictability and the elimination of uncertainty are fundamental to the nature of the product, and how the company has devised a highly effective mechanical system for organizing production.

Analysis

1. The case provides an excellent illustration of how the operation of a McDonald's retail outlet is built around the operational target of achieving close control over the efficiency of labor, and of the successful use of Taylor's five principles of Scientific Management:

(a) Responsibility for the organization of work rests with the managers and system designers at Mc's head office, not with the workers. Restaurant employees are solely concerned with implementation of pre-defined codes, procedures and responsibilities. There is a split between "brain" and "hand."

b) Use of scientific methods to define work activities; everything is precisely defined (e.g. store layout, design and layout of equipment, cooking times, shelf (or rack) life of cooked products, characteristics of raw materials, quantities of all ingredients and dressings, and day to day operations are determined by a detailed manual of instructions ranging from the maintenance of equipment to the removal of snow.)

(c) Selection: the focus is on employment of enthusiastic, pleasing young people (often students) seeking temporary work for basic wages.

(d) Training: careful instruction on basic work activities; programming of sales talk which leaves nothing to chance.

(e) Monitoring of performance: the important function of store manager and outside evaluations; all work must be performed according to plan; careful systems of evaluation in use (see the checklist in Exhibit 2.1 of Images (Page 21) for a comparative example); workers start with simple jobs and graduate to the more difficult on the basis of good work performance.

2. The case shows how McDonald's thrives on standardization and the elimination of uncertainty to produce low cost products in a uniform way. The restaurant is a kind of machine: the uniformity of product is basic to its marketing;

Big Mac's are the same all over the world. The controls on production are extremely mechanical: standardization, routinization, and precision manufacturing and service is enforced throughout. An additional point, not discussed in this case, is that the demand for uniformity also extends backwards into the supplier network: the selection and provision of beef, hamburger patties, buns and other products is also subject to rigorous control.

3. The case provides a platform for discussion about the links between mechanistic organization and the process of innovation. McDonald's is a highly innovative company. It has pioneered and executed a new approach to the provision of restaurant services, having done much to <u>create</u> the fast-food industry. How does this square <u>with</u> the mechanistic organization so evident in its day to day operations? This paradox provides an excellent vehicle for class discussion.

The answer, of course, lies in the fact that the innovation rests with the corporate staff in McDonald's head office. This is the "brain" behind the McDonald's organization. McDonald's has combined a highly innovative central office with a highly efficient system of production in its retail outlets.

4. Developing the innovation theme, important insights can be developed by posing the question: How innovative can McDonald's become? Are there limits? For example, the more product lines that are introduced, the more difficult it becomes to organize retail outlets as efficient and productive machines. Problems of co-ordination, etc. increase logarithmically as the number of product lines increase. Will the innovative character of recent years, especially in terms of adding new product lines, encounter new organizational problems if continued?

Examining this problem from a head office viewpoint, how can this problem be reconciled? How can one sustain innovative product development and marketing teams if there is a limit on the number of products that can be produced? Note that in North America much of the innovation hinges on creating a "McDonald's experience" - the innovation shapes the context rather than the hamburgers.

5. The case also provides an opportunity to discuss the corporate culture of McDonald's: to what extent do the orientations and motivations of its young employees shape the ethos of work experience in the store. Students who have worked for McDonalds are often able to share valuable insights here.

6. The case provides a platform for discussing employment relations in the retail outlets. To what extent is the competitive advantage of McDonalds dependent on its ability to pay low wages and keep prices low? What would be the reaction to an unionization of employees? Would the firm close down retail outlets threatened by this development rather than run the risk of unionization within the whole organization? To what extent is the policy of employing young mobile people with temporary affiliations a means of avoiding this risk? To what extent do employment practices contain seeds of an exploitative relation? All these questions link the case to the political aspects of organizational life.

7. Finally, the case provides an excellent platform for moving to a discussion of the organization of franchising systems generally. To what extent is the ability to franchise a product dependent on the kind of organization reflected in McDonald's? (See the class plan on the Machine Metaphor for ideas).

ACME & OMEGA (COT #79)

This case, produced by Dr. J.F. Veiga, describes events in two organizations operating at the fringe of the electronics industry in the 1950's and 1960's. Acme is a mechanistic organization with a distinctive competence in the high volume manufacture of printed circuits and their subsequent assembly. Omega is more loosely structured, and has high competence in problem solving. The case focuses on changes in the environment associated with the move from printed circuit boards to integrated circuits or electronic "chips", and the impact on the two organizations. In particular it illustrates how Acme experiences great difficulty in dealing with the new requirements, and how Omega which has hitherto lived in the shadow of Acme's high degree of efficiency, comes into its own. The case illustrates how organizational structures and management systems vary, how different organizational styles may be better suited for different organizational tasks, and raises questions with regard to the future strategies that the organizations could or should pursue. Though the case may at first seem "dated," it has major contemporary relevance.

Analysis

The case falls into four parts:

Part I: The differences between mechanistic and organic organization, and "the variety of the species."

1. The case provides an excellent launching pad for discussion about Burns and Stalker's distinctions between

mechanistic and organic organizations. Acme provides a good illustration of the mechanistic, while Omega is more loosely organized. While many students identify Omega as organic in the Burns & Stalker terminology, this is not strictly correct. It is an intermediate form of organization: Omega avoids the use of organization chart, encourages informal (rather than written) patterns of communication, but is still highly departmentalized, and most decisions are made by a top management group. In general style of organization it lies somewhere between the switchgear firm and radio and TV firm illustrated in the continuum on pages 52-53 of Images. An excellent discussion can be generated by getting students to identify where Omega falls on this continuum. There are clear differences between the styles of the two company presidents: Acme's Tyler is authoritarian and likes to run a tight ship; Omega's Rawls is much looser. How far are the two companies shaped by these two styles?

2. I use the above discussion to launch into detailed analysis of what truly organic firms are like and how they differ from firms like Omega. I also use the opportunity to discuss matrix organizations, and the varieties of these found in practice. In the process, I give a detailed and extended treatment of the continuum of organizational forms illustrated on pages 52-53 of Images and in COT #27.

3. In discussing the varieties of organization found in practice it is useful to introduce the idea that organizations are rarely uniformly mechanistic/organic, etc. and that they may vary quite considerably in terms of style and structure. This leads to a discussion of Lawrence and Lorsch's theory of differentiation and integration; how organizations must organize for "sub-environments" and "sub-tasks", while retaining an appropriate measure of integration (COT #23).

Parts II & III: Contingency theory and "good fit" between organization and environment.

Part II of the case introduces the issue of environmental change, and imposes a new task on each of the two organizations: the assembly of a prototype photocopier. It provides an excellent platform for getting students thinking about the implications of these changes for Acme & Omega and predicting likely consequences. In addition to explaining which firm will produce the best results and why, I ask students to describe in detail exactly how the two firms will deal with the new assignment. This forces them to think through the style and philosophy of organization adopted in each firm, and leads them to anticipate and predict many of the details described in Part III of the case. This helps them to see that a logic of organization is at work, unfolding in accordance with the way each firm operates, and that the features of Part III are not just coincidental.

Part III describes how Acme & Omega deal with their new assignment. Acme runs into numerous problems. Its mechanistic top-down approach creates numerous rigidities; the novelty of the task overwhelms, and creates in-fighting between departments as traditional protocol breaks down. Omega, on the other hand thrives on the novelty. Its open pattern of communications and consultative style of decision-making is ideal for tackling the task at hand. Indeed Omega engineers even spot an important error in the blueprint, and are able to point this out to the firm.

The contrasts between Acme and Omega in parts I and III of the case are dramatic. They illustrate the basic principles of contingency theory: that the most effective style of organization depends on the task being performed. This provides an opportunity for the class to discuss what style of organization works best, when, and why. I use the contrast between Parts I and III of the case to illustrate the principles of congruency and incongruency discussed in Images pp 60-65, and elaborated in COT #32. Get students to use the blank contingency diagrams in COT #78 to plot the profiles of Acme and Omega in Parts I and III of the case.

In Part I Acme is congruent with its stable task-environment; Omega is incongruent (too loosely organized for the stable environment). In Parts II and III Omega is congruent with its changing task environment; Acme is now out of line (too rigidly organized). In each phase, congruence is linked to organizational efficiency and effectiveness.

Part IV: The importance of strategy and organizational choice

Part IV poses a question? What should Acme & Omega do in the future? What advice can be given to the President of each firm regarding future survival.

I use this opportunity to introduce the importance of strategic decisions in linking organization and environment and encourage my class to develop strategies for the two firms. This leads to a discussion of the firms distinctive competencies, and the choices that need to be made with regard to organization and management. The class quickly recognizes that if Acme is to retain its present mode of organization it must recognize that its distinctive competence rests in efficient mass production. Omega's rests in innovation and problem solving. Perhaps each should specialize in these activities. This would lead Acme to search for a more stable environment that it can defend through cost-efficient production. Omega could avoid head-on competition with the Acmes of this world by building a competence for dealing with change. In each case the search will be for "good fit" between organization and environment (see COT #32 for a discussion of defender, analyzer and prospector strategies). Perhaps Acme's future rests in being a good defender, Omega's in being a good analyzer. Though effective in problem solving it is doubtful whether Omega has the competencies to compete with the truly organic or highly developed team-based organizations found in the modern electronics industry. These are the true prospectors.

This discussion of the links between strategy, environment and organization provides an excellent platform for further discussion of these issues e.g. through a focus on the Scholar Educational Product case.

SCHOLAR EDUCATIONAL PRODUCTS (COT #80)

Overview

This case presents events in Scholar Educational, a company with a solid record of success in the educational products field. It has a number of well-established product lines and consistently turns in good sales and profit results. However, the firm is facing the possibility of transformation in its environment as a result of the revolution in microelectronics: as new developments in computer technology change the whole learning process, and undermine the firm's market in the field of encyclopedias, and other traditional learning aids. The firm has vaguely sensed the possibility of this change, and established a New Products Department to investigate possible new directions. However, its commitment to the new department is rather lukewarm, and there is a real question as to whether the firm has really grasped the threat which changes in the environment present to its future viability, or whether vested interests - consciously or unconsciously - are closing the initiative down.

Analysis

1. The case raises an obvious question: How would you describe the corporate strategy pursued by Scholar Educational? This is an excellent platform for initiating discussion about how Scholar is dealing with its changing environment. Using the Miles and Snow typology presented in COT #32 the details of the case raise the question as to whether it is a defender organization trying to become an analyzer. But there is a question of their commitment to change, and the extent to which the New Products division will be given the scope to initiate required transformation. Certainly it seems that the niche occupied by Scholar is probably not sufficiently robust to defend in the long run, since encyclopedias will undoubtedly be challenged by the new technology. An environmental analysis would seem to favor an analyzer strategy which perhaps preserves the existing

strengths of the company while repositioning the firm in relation to new products. The challenge facing the firm rests in making this transition. The case provides an opportunity to perform a detailed contingency analysis using the model discussed in Chapter 3 of Images and COT #s 32 and 78. Use of this model identifies the key parameters which need to be influenced to create effective change. The pattern of incongruence is similar to that of Acme in Parts II and III of the Acme & Omega case. For example, it is clear that to cope with the new challenges of the environment Scholar will have to change many aspects of its existing structure and management system, and encourage new attitudes among its employees.

2. Why is the company not responding to the challenge? This question presents an opportunity to explore the cultural, political and unconscious factors that may be blocking change, and how Cindy Winton could be more effective in managing her contribution to the organization. How could Cindy Winton have been more successful in getting her proposals accepted? As head of the New Products Department she is a key figure in any change, and from evidence presented in the case is facing real problems. The company is "sales" and "bottom-line" oriented in a short run sense, and seems reluctant to shift from its traditional domain. The only new products it seems willing to consider those which supplement existing product lines. With the benefit of contingency insights Cindy Winton could be much more effective in using the New Products Division to spearhead change. The evidence of the case suggests that she is a long way from being successful in this. By putting ourselves in Winton's position it is possible to identify coherent strategies for change e.g. she has to gain the confidence of existing management. To what extent can she try and "sell" new product ideas in terms of their values? At present she adopts a rather abstract "missionary" approach. Perhaps there is more than she can do in terms of internal "salesmanship" and entrepreneurship e.g. "talk in the language of sales and bottom line"; select the projects to move in ways that will gain their confidence; move gradually from supplements to existing product lines to the introduction of completely new ideas.

This line of investigation would identify different strategies open to Winton such as the idea of trying to canvas support from key actors in the organization prior to making her proposal, but would ultimately draw attention to the basic values and infrastructure of this company. At base, it is necessary to recognize that at present it has little innovative potential. It is truly a sales oriented company, that is oriented towards short-run bottom-line concerns, and a major "cultural" transformation of the organization is going to be necessary. Given this scenario, there is probably little

that Winton can do as a single actor to achieve the desired
change. But if she can build an appropriate coalition which
encourages the organization to take a close and hard look at
itself and the environment, then there are possibilities, even
though we would have to conclude that there are few grounds
for optimism.

3. The above discussion inevitably shows that there are
important "cultural" and "political" aspects to the case that
can be examined in detail. Do people feel threatened? Is
there a gender bias? What is the status of the resistance to
change? There's no hard evidence, but plenty of room for
speculation.

4. Finally, the case can be used to dramatize the true
requirements of innovation. Scholar is not a company that has
attempted to develop and institutionalize innovation to any
real degree - a contrast that emerges with great force when
compared with organizations like 3M and Apple Computer,
discussed later in these notes.

THE CHANGING STRUCTURE OF FINANCIAL SERVICES (COT #81)

Use this case to illustrate some of the major transformations
occurring in established sectors of society, and the need for new
ways of thinking about the external environment, strategy, etc.
(See COT #s 30, 31, 34, 35). Its purpose is to provide exemplars
and a base for general discussion: see the discussion questions
at the end of the case.

ORGANIZATIONS OFTEN OBSTRUCT LEARNING (COT #82)

Overview

This short case from Jay Galbraith's work illustrates the
difficulties faced by a small electronics firm which finds a
solution to a design problem, but is unable to get the design
improvement accepted and implemented. Excellent for illustrating
the pathologies of bureaucratized organizations, especially when
used alongside the case of Product X (COT #83). Has close links
with the Acme and Omega case.

Analysis

The company, a small electronics firm with 1,200 employees faces
a turbulent environment. The firm's president sees the need for
innovation and provides appropriate resources, but the company
fails to deliver. In analyzing the reasons why, we learn much
about the problems of organizational learning (See Images pp. 84-
95):

1. Bureaucratization builds boundaries; it fragments
intelligence; it often makes integrated action difficult.
Many examples of this are found in the case. Divisions within
the company have become deep and rigid. Departments do not
work together in an effective way; they often try and
"protect their turf" and resent encroachment. The young field
engineer who produces a much needed innovation experiences all
these problems. To be effective he has to be protected from
the negative attitudes and reactions of his colleagues.

2. Rules create inflexibility; like bureaucratic boundaries
they often create barriers to effective action. Company
policies and rigid reward systems get in the way of producing
the required response.

3. Institutional divisions become "political" divisions.
"Turf protection", a sense of prerogative, and a sense of
threat, lead the engineers that should have solved the
problem to block the initiative.

4. The case provides an excellent platform for discussing
Galbraith's concept of the "innovating organization" and of
how management can help institutionalize processes that
encourage innovation eg. the need for sponsorship, product
championship, flexibility in funding and reward systems (See
COT #49 on 3M).

PRODUCT X (COT #83)

Overview

A short case from the work of Argyris and Schon illustrating how
organizations often obstruct flows of information, making it
impossible for the organization to learn from its mistakes and
engage in adaptative action. Excellent when used in conjunction
with COT #82.

Analysis

This case can be used to trigger multifaceted discussion on
impediments to organizational learning. I use it to highlight
the following:

(a) There are often structural impediments to learning: many
of the structural arrangements within the organization in
question (eg. hierarchy) work in ways that actually block
flows of important information.

(b) Many distortions are often linked to processes of
accountability: systems of accountability are linked with
patterns of protective behavior.

(c) There are often _political_ impediments to learning: many of the distortions in this case are associated with the process of "covering up", avoiding "looking bad" and protecting one's personal position.

The case is very direct and straightforward, and provides an ideal platform for linking to a more generalized discussion about how organizations promote "single-loop" learning, block "double-loop" learning, etc..

SELF-ORGANIZATION/AUTONOMOUS WORK GROUPS/HOLOGRAPHIC ORGANIZATION (COT #s 46, 47, & Volvo video)

It's necessary to have practical illustrations of the approaches to "holographic organization" discussed in Chapter 4 of Images. I use the following:

COT #47 discussing team-based manufacturing at Digital Equipment.

COT #47 on Magna International. This provides a nice illustration of the "whole in the parts" design philosophy. Magna grows by spawning relatively self-contained factories and companies.

To create a visual focus for discussion I use a video on Volvo's Kalmar plant, illustrating their approach to the design of autonomous work groups (The Video has been produced by Volvo as part of its P.R. activities). There are other videos on autonomous work groups or group technology that can also serve your needs - check your film library. Whatever the video you choose, use it in a way that highlights the contrast between the group technology typical of the Kalmar plant and Digital's approach to manufacturing and traditional assembly line technology. The holographic properties discussed in Chapter 4 of Images (requisite variety, redundant functions, learning to learn and minimum critical specification) are clearly evident in the operations of these work teams, which are designed to promote a high degree of self-organization.

One can use the discussion of holographic organization to launch a discussion of its impact on the culture and politics of an organization. For example, how does team-based organization influence power relations on the factory floor? What is the impact of this kind of technology on the power of the unions? Does "team consciousness" replace "union consciousness"? Is there a political agenda behind management's attempt to introduce group technology? This line of questioning helps to illustrate two different interpretations that can be placed on the move towards principles of self organization and group-technology, and the very real political dilemmas faced by labour unions.

ARNOLD: THE PARADOX OF CREATIVITY (<u>COT</u> #84)

A simple "tickler" designed to stimulate discussion about the potential conflict between the demands for creativity and everyday organization. Use the discussion questions to explore this issue.

<u>UNDERSTANDING THE CULTURE OF YOUR ORGANIZATION</u> (<u>COT</u> #85)

Use this exercise to get students to take a close look at the culture of an organization with which they are familiar. It can be used to analyze or think about the corporate cultures illustrated in the videos of organizations shown in the course (e.g. Apple, 3M).

There are various refinements that can be introduced. For example, with practitioners it's useful to get them to describe their corporate culture <u>now</u> (showing the principal cultures and sub-cultures), and as they would like it to be (say in 10 years time).

3M (<u>COT</u> #49 and video case)

This reading on innovation at 3M can be supplemented with the video of decision-making in 3M featured in Peter's and Waterman's <u>In Search of Excellence</u> program. The video focuses on the development of two 3M products: "Post-it" labels and laser discs, and illustrates how 3M institutionalizes a form of lawlessness and entrepreneurial activity to foster new ideas, and new products. Considerable attention is given to the need for organizational champions that will pioneer and steer innovative ideas through the organization.

The case is excellent for illustrating how strategy and initiative often evolve through a combination of unplanned events and systematic experimentation. For example the way in which 3M convinced their marketing department about the viability of their non-adhesive "post-it" stickers is excellent in illustrating this action bias. It provides an excellent illustration of how innovation emerges, as commitment builds around a project. It illustrates a truly learning-orientated organization (an excellent contrast with the organizations featured in <u>COT</u> #s 80, 82, 83).

The video is also excellent for providing students with an opportunity to document and describe the dominant 3M culture (for example, using the exercise in <u>COT</u> #85). It provides an

excellent basis for comparison with other video cases to be
described later (e.g. Apple Computer, Mary Kay Cosmetics).

APPLE COMPUTER (COT #57 and video case)

Overview

Apple has undergone major changes in recent years passing from
the youthful organization led by Steve Jobs into a more
professionalized, steady, mature organization under John Sculley.
A great focus for examining innovation, culture, politics and
change. Use the In Search of Excellence video focussing on
Apple's Macintosh team led by Jobs and COT #57 to illustrate
these points. The Apple video of their 1984 Annual General
Meeting (produced by Apple's P.R. Department) can act as a
valuable supplementary resource if available.

Analysis

1. Innovation and Self-organization. I often open discussion
of the In Search of Excellence video with the following
question: What are the secret's of Apple's success on the
Macintosh project? What organizing principles are reflected
in this case? This line of inquiry leads to the
identification of many issues, one of which focuses on the
fact that organization does not always rest in formal
structures; it may lie in the ethos and spirit that pervades
the organization. Jobs helped create an innovative
environment, leading by example, building around people and
abilities rather than roles, encouraging self-organization,
self-management, and risk-taking, acting as coach,
cheer-leader and encourager of champions. By reflecting on
the nature of the Macintosh project students are able to
grasp the reality of organic management and the alternatives
to bureaucratic organization.

The situation at Apple can be usefully contrasted with the
situation at 3M, to illustrate that successful innovative
organizations often vary in approach. 3M's approach to
innovation is much more institutionalized than Apple's under
Jobs. We learn much about the organization of innovation by
focusing on similarities and differences between the two
companies.

2. Corporate culture. There is so much in this video to
illustrate the symbolic side of organizational life and how
successful organization hinges on the creation of shared
meaning. I develop this in relation to the theme of managing
innovation (successful innovating companies build around
shared values and commitments to an incredible degree), and
also in relation to the analysis of culture more generally,

using COT #85 as a supporting exercise. Here again the contrasts with 3M create a great vehicle for exploring the nature of corporate culture, and the detailed means through which it is constructed and sustained on a day to day basis.

If possible, try supplementing the In Search of Excellence video with the one on Apple's 1984 AGM. The culture of Apple under Jobs emerges even more strongly: youthful, exuberant, fun-loving, arrogant, noisy, anarchic, aggressive, built on the David-Goliath relationship between Apple and IBM. A great illustration of the impact of a charismatic leader on an organization. A great basis for illustrating how the young company became trapped by its youthful inexperience: ignoring the requirements of the business world; producing the computer that they want to produce rather than what the market needs; laying the basis for the eventual clash between Jobs and Scully, and the company's evolution into a new stage of development.

3. The Politics of organization. Jobs' clash with Sculley and eventual departure from Apple (see COT #57) raises intriguing questions regarding the politics of the organization generally. To what extent was the isolation of the Macintosh team a factor generating political problems? To what extent is this a problem with intrapreneurship generally (the Macintosh team is often seen as a model or intrapreneurship). Innovative departments and people are often rejected by their host organization, so many general principles are involved here. The departure of Jobs also raises questions relating to potential clashes between personal, career and task objectives, the importance of clashing visions, coalitions, etc., in the evolution of corporate politics.

4. Organizational life-cycles. The case also raises questions relating to life-cycle theories of organization and whether Apple's maturation under a new leader was an inevitable line of development.

MARY KAY COSMETICS (THE PINK PANTHER)

Overview

To illustrate the concept of corporate culture even further I like to use a video-case (from the Sixty Minutes program, titled The Pink Panther) which focuses on the philosophy and culture of Mary Kay Cosmetics. It describes and illustrates the core values around which this direct sales organization builds, with a particular focus on the corporation's annual convention at Dallas. Excellent for providing an extreme example of how an organization can be managed through shared values and beliefs (the management of meaning). The video is guaranteed to provoke discussion, not least because of Mary Kay's views of the role of women in society.

Analysis

There are many themes that can be brought out in discussion:

(a) Cult or corporate culture? A common reaction to the video case is that it illustrates an extreme quasi-religious organization. Parallels are often drawn with the Rev. Moon's Unification Church. This often raises the issue of whether the corporation is manipulating and exploiting its employees. Against this interpretation, others see in Mary Kay's philosophy all the requirements of Maslow's "higher need" motivation: Mary Kay's success rests in her ability to create fulfilling lives and growing self-respect among her employees.

(b) Organizational symbolism and the management of meaning! The video is packed with illustrations of how symbols, slogans, rituals and other social processes combine to create a cohesive pattern of shared meaning. The idea that Mary Kay is "managing meaning" and helping people make a reality provides an interesting twist to explanations drawing on Maslow's theory. The same data are interpreted in a different way.

(c) On a scale measuring the "visibility" of a corporate culture (1=low, 10=high) the Mary Kay corporation would score a 10. It is an extreme case. This can be used as an interesting way to promote more general discussion about the nature of corporate culture. For example, I use the idea of the 1 to 10 scale to draw attention to corporate cultures that are all but invisible, because in contrast with Mary Kay, they are very low key. Using this dichotomy between the invisible day to day aspects of a corporate culture and the gaudy glitter of Mary Kay, I get students to identify the corporate cultures of mundane organizations, using the framework presented in COT #85. I also use the Mary Kay example to initiate discussion about cross national comparisons of corporate culture: Mary Kay could only happen in America!

(d) The video presents an excellent platform for moving to a systematic comparison of corporate cultures. Using the values, rituals, vision, language and ethos of Mary Kay as a starting point, compare and contrast the cultures of Apple, 3M, IBM, etc. etc. Use the framework in COT #85 and the ideas in COT 51 as a means of doing this.

(e) Finally, building on the theme of whether Mary Kay is a cult-like organization, it is easy to initiate discussion of the relationship between corporate culture, and corporate politics, and the links between power and the management of meaning.

The case thus contains provocative material that can explore many aspects of the cultural and political metaphors.

DISCOVERY TOYS

There is an excellent video that can be used to illustrate some of the unconscious factors that can shape corporate culture. It focuses on Discovery Toys, and is contained in a video called The Entrepreneurs, Nathan/Tyler Productions, 1986.

The video focuses on the founder of the company, and produces a vivid illustration of how her preoccupation with control shapes her management style and impact on the organization. Listen to the metaphors she uses to describe her company, and her responsibility for her corporate family!

PERFECTION OR BUST (COT #86)

Overview

An excellent illustration of how corporate culture hinges on the definition of a reality or "the management of meaning". The case provides many illustrations of how symbols and language can shape the ethos of an organization. It also shows how an organization can become trapped by its culture. Design Inc. eventually carries the burden of its demands for perfection, allowing a point of principle to have negative repercussions throughout the organization.

Analysis

1. What has gone wrong? It is worth examining the reasons in some detail.

(a) Has Klee simply latched onto a superficial interpretation of the idea that it is possible to create a corporate culture, set out on this path and is now running into problems? Perhaps he is guided by a superficial interpretation of popular books on corporate culture. He has certainly created a vision and message with great potential: the problem is how to sustain it on an ongoing basis?

(b) Do some of the problems in sustaining the corporate ethos stem from the fact that the agency's reputation for excellence is generated internally rather than externally? While Art's employees may believe in their distinctiveness,

employees in competitive agencies may be seeing them as
underpaid employees living in a dream world (and sending
this message to them on the industry grapevine?). This kind
of clashing opinion often arises within an organization. In
this case we find it between organizations.

(c) Is the apparent demise of the agency linked to the
unsatisfied career and personal interests of staff,
symbolized in the departure of the top lay-out artist?
Similar tensions are still present in the agency, and they
may well work their way to the surface in time.

(d) Are there psychoanalytic factors at work in this case?
What is the hidden significance of Klee's search for
perfection? Why is it allowed to influence the organization
in such a complete way? Do psychoanalytic factors account
for the way in which the corporate culture becomes a trap?
Certainly it seems that the search for perfection is
immobilizing many aspects of the firm's current operations.
Many organizations suffer a similar fate as they become
trapped and constrained by corporate values.

Any one or combination of the above factors may explain the
current problems being faced by the firm.

2. The points identified above provide an excellent point of
departure for examining the factors that make for successful
and unsuccessful corporate cultures in more general terms.
For example, the case of Design Inc. has many points in
common with success stories such as those of Apple Computer
and Mary Kay (see CASENOTES on these videos) and Tandem (COT
#54). What are the crucial factors making for success and
failure? Considerable insight can be generated by directing
class discussion along this line of inquiry.

3. What advice could be given to Klee to help make Design
Inc. more effective? (Note that some will dispute that this
is necessary. The firm is still doing well, and Klee may be
achieving exactly what he wants - see point 4 below). Here
are some relevant points:

(a) Should Klee give more attention to the relationship
between Design Inc. and its environment? For example, he
seems to be treating his organization as a closed system.
Klee is insular rather than outward looking. He seems to
make little attempt to embody new challenges and ideas as he
goes along. At a minimum it seems that he needs to find a
way of creating a dynamic inflow and outflow of talent to
achieve and sustain the "academy" image? Should the agency
follow a prospector strategy, rather than try to defend its
niche? As it stands the company is in danger of atrophying.

(b) Would Klee benefit from a better knowledge of ideas about holographic organization to realize his ideal? His approach to management seems quite mechanistic. Note the links between Design Inc. and the Multicom case discussed in Chapter 10 of _Images_. The points relating to holographic organization in Multicom apply to Design Inc as well. Certainly, it would seem that Klee should recognize that the agency can only realize its vision by being innovative and "cutting edge" in design. It would be appropriate for him to manage for innovation in a proactive way.

(c) The above point is important in emphasizing that culture may not be enough. It's one thing to help shape a culture; its quite another to organize in a way that can sustain it over time. The principles on holographic organization may be of help here.

d) Does he need to give more attention to the personal strains and tensions underlying staff involvement? Perhaps he should be doing more to balance the "needs" of employees.

4. Finally, the case raises a host of issues in relation to the links between culture and politics. On the surface this is a case about corporate culture, but it is also about corporate politics as well.

Klee's agency is making a good profit. Is he just "selling a bill of goods", using "perfection or bust" as a way of reducing salaries, and tying people into a system that furthers his interests? A case can be made for the idea Design Inc. is doing very nicely as far as Klee is concerned. This issue can be developed to initiate a debate about the links between culture, the management of meaning, corporate politics and ideology, etc.

The case thus provides an interesting focus on the cultural, political and psychodynamic aspects of organization. Any one of these issues can provide a framework for analysis. A good case study for helping to illustrate relations between culture, politics and the unconscious.

THE CREATION AND DESTRUCTION OF THE ORDER OF MARIA THERESA (COT #87)

This case presents an excellent short description of the development and destruction of an organizational sub-unit motivated and managed through shared values and norms, rather than rules and procedures. Maria Theresa succeeds in building a highly cohesive sub-culture - working around official rules, self-organizing, exercising initiative, enjoying work, and in the process, creating a strong customer orientation and high level of work performance. The unit manages to dodge the watchful eye of the organization's control and evaluation systems, to preserve its mode of operation.

But when Maria Theresa leaves, everything changes. Her successor Vincent Macmurdo introduces a formal, rule-orientated style of management which erodes the informal culture. The sub-culture breaks down; self-organizing initiatives are eliminated; the service orientation declines; staff become increasingly dissatisfied, and are eventually fired.

Use the discussion questions at the end of the case to bring out the above points, with a focus on the following:

1. How one can build self-organizing capacities around natural abilities and motivations; self-organization emerges as a natural quality.

2. How management through values and norms often conflicts with management through rules (compare the example from Bill Ouchi's work, Images, P. 94).

3. Different managerial styles and mindsets (e.g. Maria Theresa vs Macmurdo).

4. How factors relating to holographic, cultural and political metaphors are inter-twined.

Note the parallels between this case, and that documented by Alvin Gouldner in his books Wildcat Strike (1954) and Patterns of Industrial Bureaucracy (1954). The case illustrates a process found in the experience of many organizations.

SINK OR SWIM: REFLECTIONS ON A CORPORATE TRAINING PROGRAM (COT #88)

This case provides an "inside look" at a corporate training program from the standpoint of a disillusioned employee. An excellent illustration of how training programs result in corporate rituals designed to communicate and affirm key values while "filtering" and identifying employees who fit the corporate ethos.

Use the case as the basis for a general discussion to raise the following points:

1. The role played by training programs and other socializing devices in the formation of corporate culture.

2. The issue of whether the program is an intimidation ritual?

3. Issues relating to politics and power, and the manipulative aspects of trying to shape corporate culture.

4. Ethical concerns: Was the stress created by the program immoral, as the narrator of the case suggests?

5. To what extent does this kind of program contribute to the workaholism discussed in COT #69?

THE NOMIZU SAKE COMPANY (COT #89)

The episode presented in this case provides a springboard for discussing cross cultural differences. The Japanese and American staff of the Sake company share different values and beliefs and subscribe to different norms. The different sets of values undermine each other, creating many organizational problems. The cultural problems are completely mishandled, and Wendy Suzuki is made a scapegoat.

Use the case to explore the following points:

1. The cross-cultural differences in organizational behavior, and the problems created in organizations where people from different backgrounds have to work with each other. (Link to COT #50)

2. If the Japanese believe that everyone loses face if a person makes an error, how should James Jr. have managed Kawate's anger about the tasting room slur? Shouldn't James have apologized and accepted blame on behalf of the whole organization?

3. Why did James make Suzuki a scapegoat? Is there unconscious anger being played out here, or is James simply playing a Western style of politics to get out of a difficult situation?

FORTRESS INSURANCE (COT #90)

This case focuses on the success and failure of an insurance company that embarks on a new market-oriented relationship with its environment. On the advice of outside consultants this very conservative, traditional firm recruits Bill Storm to head a new marketing department. A maverick, and an aggressive personality, he recruits people with flair and imagination and succeeds in building a cohesive department that produces wonderful results. The department has high visibility, and becomes an important step on the road to a successful career. Gradually, traditional people with traditional values begin to have an impact on the department, undermining its effectiveness. Storm loses influence and control, and eventually leaves the organization with the establishment firmly in control of the marketing function.

Analysis

This case is excellent for illustrating issues relating to corporate culture and sub-culture, the problems of integrating deviant sub- cultures within the total organization, and the politics of control. Here are some of the important points:

1. The case presents a vivid illustration of a clash between corporate culture and sub-culture, in the form of an "old guard" dominated by traditional values and mind-sets, and a "new guard" committed to very different values and styles of organizational life.

2. The case illustrates how the transformation of an organization often involves a transformation of core values. In its original state Fortress is completely out of touch with its environment. The new marketing department breathes life into the organization. But traditional values overcome the new spirit, bringing the deviant department back into line. And as a result, the organization begins to atrophy again.

3. The case raises important questions about the dynamics of culture and counter-culture. Is the process whereby the old-guard gain control a product of cultural inertia and an inability to change? Or is it the result of more active processes of political control, or unconscious resistances to change?

4. The politics of control evident in the case are worthy of detailed examination. Does the culture of the marketing department break down because of unintended infiltration by people with different values? Or was it eroded as a result of deliberate policy? Was the "old guard" within Fortress threatened by the nature and style of the new department? Did they see it as a challenge to traditional beliefs, power relations, and career paths? Was it deliberately controlled and infiltrated? Was George Tight's appointment within the marketing department strategically planned with this end in mind? Perhaps the powerful executives running this firm could not or would not tolerate with cultural "deviancy", even though it was highly successful. We do not have the data to answer these questions in detail, but they are raised by the circumstances of the case, and provide the basis for valuable understandings of the politics of control, especially in relation to the management of culture and sub-culture. George Tight occupied a key strategic role in the management of meaning.

5. The case raises important questions with regard to the actions and policies that could have helped sustain the success of the marketing department and the total organization. I find it helpful to examine this from two vantage points: that of the CEO, and that of Bill Storm:

(a) What could the CEO have done to sustain the effectiveness of the marketing department?

(i) Appreciate the importance of the corporate sub-culture that developed within the marketing department: it is central to their style of organization.

(ii) Recognize that the corporation is in the grip of traditional values, and give attention to the way they can be allowed to evolve and change.

(iii) Recognize the importance of differentiation and integration. Contingency theory tells us that different units need to be differentiated to meet the tasks posed by different sub-environments. There is thus a rationale for the marketing department being differentiated from the rest of the firm. But there is also a need to see that it is re-integrated. For example, through use of intermediaries that "see both sides"; through orchestration and sponsorship at high levels within the organization that can help get marketing accepted; by getting Storm to temper deviance from an external standpoint; and by finding ways of making the flamboyance of the marketing department less visible. Clearly, the integration of the marketing department is not being managed in an effective way.

(iv) Building on the above point, it is necessary to realize that the transformation of this organization is the core issue. It needs to be carefully handled in a differentiated and integrated way. More could be done to create a sense of shared vision and direction for the whole, and how the new marketing department fits into this broader scheme of things.

(v) Finally, there are important aspects to the political management of this organization. Is the CEO a part of the "old guard mentality"? If so, how can he break free, or how can the company create a new initiative that is independent of him? How can the "old guard" be managed in a way that will promote change? How can Storm's brashness and enthusiasm be managed as a constructive force?

(b) What could Storm have done to make the marketing

department and its relations with the wider organization more effective?

(i) Clearly, more could have been done to temper the impact of the marketing "culture" on the rest of the organization. Knowledge of the principle of differentiation and integration would have helped Storm appreciate the managerial challenge facing both himself and the chief executive.

(ii) An awareness of the dynamics of the culture-counter culture relationship could have made him more aware of the "threat from within" the organization. Did he realize the importance of "protecting" his department and avoiding the infiltration that occurred?

(iii) He could have done more to manage boundaries. By exploring the interface between marketing and the rest of the organization he could have moderated the negative impact of his department, while sustaining its distinctiveness and strength. A better knowledge of external linkages would have allowed him to assess broader dynamics of the situation, whether the split in orientations and values was superficial or fundamental, and whether the situation was manageable, or so politicized that he was bound to lose any attempt at maintaining the position of his department. Maybe the gulf with the old guard could have been bridged, e.g. by building coalitions and support for his unit and its ethos in key places, educating others about what he was doing, etc.. For the most part Storm was insular and egocentric. Ideas about boundary management could have led to a much more proactive style for consolidating his department's early achievements.

(iv) A greater awareness of the politics of control could have helped Storm counter Tight's initiatives. There is much that he could do to improve his political awareness, the role of gatekeeping, management of meaning etc.

This case is excellent in focusing diverse insights derived from organismic, cultural and political metaphors. Note the links with the Scholar Educational Products case.

RAINBOW FINANCIAL SERVICES (COT #91)

Overview

This case addresses some of the organizational changes taking place in the financial services industry (see COT #81 for elaboration). CEO Redding is changing Rainbow - structurally, culturally, politically. An excellent case for illustrating how these elements of organization are inter-twined.

Analysis

Try bringing out the following points:

1. Rainbow is undergoing cultural change - from an organization dominated by tradition, steadiness, paternalism, detail, to one based on a more competitive market orientation with a desire to exploit new opportunities (Compare Fortress Insurance COT #90).

2. Structural and political changes are being "engineered" along with this change - departments and services are being reorganized; key people are being replaced; "bearers" and symbols of the new order are rising within the organization.

3. The changes, especially the removal of Art Brown, are being interpreted by some people from a political perspective where gender issues are paramount. Is the focus on the fact that Golden is a woman going to obscure the changes that are really taking place? What dynamic underlies this? Are associates of the "old guard" unconsciously deflecting attention from the main issues and their inability to adjust? This often occurs in organizations undergoing major change.

4. Evaluate the role of CEO Redding as a means of highlighting how major organizational change requires a major shift in vision and values. Compare Redding with the CEO in Fortress Insurance. Comparisons between the CEO's in the two cases can prove highly instructive.

THE UNIVERSITY AS A POLITICAL SYSTEM (COT #92)

The aim here is to illustrate how the model of interests (task, career and extra-mural), conflict and power discussed in Images (Ch. 6) can be used to analyze organizational politics in a concrete way. The exercise can be applied to any organization: just encourage people to examine relations between the principal groups and coalitions. I like to use the university as an example on university courses because students are well aware of the politics of university life from their own experience, even though they don't understand it in these terms. The case thus provides the basis for a good learning experience. (Get them to do the analysis prior to class). Typically, our discussion ends up by developing the kind of model presented on the following page.

The advantage of building this case from the student's experience is that it shows them the reality of politics in their own situation. They all have first hand experience of the interests, conflict and power plays that occur between the three groups identified in the analysis. This exercise can help any person in any organization diagnose the main political interactions shaping organizational life.

	STUDENTS	ACADEMICS	ADMINISTRATORS
INTERESTS	e.g. -Interesting courses -Grades -A good time	-Research -Teaching -Administration -A good time(?) -An easy life(?) -Promotion	-Administration of systems (propagation of rules?) -Efficiency -Faculty needs -Student needs -An easy life(?) -Promotion
CONFLICTS	e.g.-Faculty-Student over assessments -Student-student competition	-Academic-Administrative -Inter-departmental/policy conflicts -Faculty-student over grades, time priorities -Research vs teaching priorities -Minimize rules	-Inter-personal -Inter-departmental -Academic-administrative
POWER	e.g. -Academic abilities -Teaching evaluations -Capacities for collective voice and collective action -Use of rules and regulations for own ends	-Professional expertise -Control of grades -Formal authority -Short duration of courses -Academic autonomy	-Control of procedures and scheduling -Control of resources -Critical dependencies e.g. for providing good service to faculty

GLOBAL INC. A ROLEPLAY

This roleplay is designed to illustrate the interaction between task, career, and extramural (personal) interests in a group decision-making situation, and the power-plays that can occur.

Instructions

1. Allow up to 3/4 hour for the roleplay, and 3/4 hour for analysis and discussion.

2. The exercise can be done in a fishbowl setting before the whole class, or in groups.

3. Get each person involved to play their role (keeping the instructions/script confidential to themselves), to simulate the actual meeting (scripts for each person follow).

4. Follow the role-play with a class analysis; don't let participants reveal their roles until the end of the analysis.

5. Where the role-play is performed in a fish-bowl setting, get different members of the class to focus on a specific person in the meeting; get the rest of the class to observe in general.

6. In the analysis, get the class to bring out their interpretations of what happened. End the analysis by getting the five role players to read their actual scripts. Make sure that Steve Elliot reads his last!

Analysis

1. Given this is a free-wheeling roleplay, discussion can develop in a number of different directions. A lot of real-time" analysis is thus required, to relate specific episodes to underlying principles. However, the roles do create a structure that shapes the meeting, especially in terms of the interaction between the task, career, and extramural interests of the role players. For example, the Table on the following page gives an overall view of how the role-play is set up; the actual role-play may introduce new twists and orientations.

The conflicts that this structure of underlying interests brings out will become obvious in the role play. Note the coalition structures that develop, and how different interests shape the course of discussion. Watch how the course of the meeting changes when the agenda changes from the program itself, to who is to present the proposal to the Board. Coalitions change!

2. The role-play will bring out important power plays. Watch for them and document specific examples - to show the class how meetings are shaped by power dynamics. Here are some obvious examples that may apply:

- coalition building
- confrontation vs building support/consensus
- use of chairperson's role
- verbal domination: talking a lot; raised voices.
- management of meaning: e.g. changing definition of what the issue "really is", invention of facts; presentation of cogent argument.

Note how the power-plays change along with the issue under discussion. The issue of who is to present the proposal to the Board usually breaks down the early alliance between Jane Hudson and Louise Sadowski.

A great role-play for illustrating the politics of organization!

(Many thanks to Linda Smircich for her help in developing this exercise!)

TYPE OF INTEREST

	TASK	CAREER	EXTRAMURAL
Jane Hudson (Human Resources Dept.)	In favour of employment of more women to promote company's wider mission and image.	Wants to present proposal to CEO and the board.	Wants a quick meeting.
Louise Sadowski (Public Relations and Corporate Communications)	In favour of proposal will help company's image. Will give P.R. department a concrete issue to work on.	Wants to present the proposal	Strong personal beliefs favouring advancement of women
Joe McNamara (Production)	Sees a lot of disadvantages for the Production Dept.	Gripe with Louise Sardowski. Wants to present proposal. Interested in his status and visibility in the company.	
Bill Furillo (Finance)	Wants to keep costs down, and to slow the process down.		Against the women's movement in business context.
Steve Elliott (Marketing)			Interested in dating Jane Hudson.

"Script" for Jane Hudson

GLOBAL ROLEPLAY

(Please don't show your role instructions to anyone.)

You are Jane Hudson, Director of Human Resources and Personnel Development of the Global Corporation. The CEO and President of the Corporation, Mr. Zane, has asked you to make a policy recommendation: Should the company have as one of the major thrusts in its FIVE YEAR PLAN a commitment to the hiring and promotion of women?

You've had preliminary discussions with your four colleagues who have been asked to participate in this decision. But today is the day for the final decision about the recommendation. There are two agenda items for the meeting you have called.

1) To decide yes or no, should the company have as one element in its Five Year Plan a commitment to the hiring and promotion of women?

2) Who should present the recommendation to the CEO and Board of Directors at the upcoming Policy Review Meeting?

You personally have no doubts about the recommendations to be made: of course Global should articulate its commitment to women. Global prides itself on its image of progressiveness. An affirmative action "plan" in the five year plan is totally congruent with the strategic vision and corporate slogan "leadership in technology for the improvement of society". What is more important to leadership and improvement in society than a commitment to women and the contributions they can make through corporations?

In any event you are extremely interested in being the one who brings the policy recommendation to the Board. It will be great for your visibility and career. It's not very often that a Director of Human Resources and Personnel Development gets to make a presentation to the Board and you don't want to let this opportunity pass you by.

You've scheduled the meeting to last an hour, but you're hoping the group can make its decisions quickly.

"Script" for Bill Furillo

GLOBAL ROLEPLAY

(Please don't show your role instructions to anyone).

You are Bill Furillo, VP of Finance of the Global Corporation. You have been asked by Jane Hudson, Director of Human Resources and Personnel Development to participate in formulating a policy recommendation. Should the company have as one of the major thrusts in its FIVE YEAR PLAN a commitment to the hiring and promotion of women?

You have high regard for the work Jane Hudson is doing in Human Resources. She's the first Personnel Director to have kept the training division within budget in ten year's time. And she's a poised articulate spokesperson for the human side of the business. But this Affirmative Action "plan" is way out of line. Women's liberation is not part of the job of American business.

In any event you bet no one has bothered to consider the financial implications of this policy. It's apt to be very expensive. You'd like to see this whole process slowed down somewhat until attention is paid to the financials. And you're sure at least McNamara in Production will see things the way you do.

"Script" for Louise Sadowski

GLOBAL ROLEPLAY

(Please don't show your role instructions to anyone.)

You are Louise Sadowski, Director of Public Relations and Corporate Communications of the Global Corporation. You have been asked by Jane Hudson, Director of Human Resources and Personnel Development to participate in formulating a policy recommendation. Should the company have as one of the major thrusts in its FIVE YEAR PLAN a commitment to the hiring and promotion of women?

As far as you're concerned there is no question. You think one of the reasons Global has the image of progressiveness in the industry is due to the presence of a few extremely competent women in high and visible places (although not high enough or visible enough for your tastes!). You would like to see affirmative action commitment made not only because it's congruent with your personal philosophy and the company's self image as a leader in the industry, but because you have already been thinking of the tremendous public relations campaign you could launch. This campaign would give your people a chance to go on the offensive to promote something socially good instead of spending so much time on the defensive. Your office has been under a lot of pressure lately from outside groups and the morale of your staff is suffering.

You are a little apprehensive about this meeting because Mr. McNamara VP of Production will be there. Unfortunately, there is a little "bad blood" between the two of you. You did a story in the corporate magazine on the Quality Circles program in Production and he feels you didn't give him enough credit for the program's success. You still don't understand how he can want to take credit for the wonderful ideas his people are coming up with!

Once the policy recommendation is formed you would very much like to be the one who brings it to the Board's upcoming Policy Review Meeting, or at least be sure to be a joint presenter. It will be great for your visibility and career. You have made several formal presentations to the Board of Directors before and you know you could do a good job to persuade any reluctant Board Members (mostly 50-ish white males) of the value of such a policy.

Ms. Hudson has scheduled this meeting for an hour, but you hope it's over quickly because you have a lunch date.

"Script" for Joe McNamara

GLOBAL ROLEPLAY

(Please don't show your role instructions to anyone)

You are Joe McNamara, VP of Production of the Global Corporation. You have been asked by Jane Hudson, Director of Human Resources and Personnel Development to participate in formulating a policy recommendation. Should the company have as one of the major thrusts in its FIVE YEAR PLAN a commitment to the hiring and promotion of women?

You can hardly believe you are being called away from your busy schedule to participate in more corporate naval gazing. After all Global already has a fine reputation for progressiveness in the industry. Look at the Quality Circles program you installed so successfully. The company has already done more than enough to be considered a good corporate citizen. Furthermore an affirmative action policy would be very difficult for you to comply with. There's not much place for women in the production area. To try to bring women in and give them unfair advantages sounds very risky. Just imagine the flack you'll catch from the supervisors and foremen. And Hudson will probably suggest to Mr. Zane, CEO and President, that affirmative action goals be part of all executive's formal ratings. You can see your appraisal suffering simply because women won't work out in Production. That's not fair.

You are glad that Ms. Sadowski Director of Public Relations and Corporate Communications will be at the meeting. You have a bone to pick with her. She did a story in the corporate magazine on the Quality Circles program in Production and she barely mentioned you! How does she think that makes you look?

Well you're not going to continue to be "Mr. Invisible" for long. Once the policy about women is formed, whichever way it goes, you will definitely be the one who brings it to the Board's upcoming Policy Review Meeting. You need that visibility in front of the Board of Directors, and you may be able to impact how it's handled.

"Script" for Steve Elliot

GLOBAL ROLEPLAY

(Please don't show your role instructions to anyone.)

You are Steve Elliot, Vice President of Marketing of the Global Corporation. You have been asked by Jane Hudson, Director of Human Resources and Personnel Development to participate in formulating a <u>policy recommendation.</u> Should the company have as one of the major thrusts in its FIVE YEAR PLAN a commitment to the hiring and promotion of women?

Quite frankly you don't care one way or the other about this issue. As far as you see it the "hey day" of affirmative action is long past. Your department has a fair representation of women and minorities already. But you think Mr. Zane, the CEO and President of Global would like to see it as policy, because it would look good to the media and fit the company's progressive image. Fine with you. It's no "skin off your nose" as the saying goes.

What you're more interested in is Jane Hudson. She's an attractive and competent woman. You find yourself looking for excuses to stop by her office. You're glad for this opportunity to meet her. Maybe there's a chance she'll be willing to go out with you, now that your divorce is final.

HOW POLITICIZED IS YOUR ORGANIZATION? (COT #94)

This simple exercise is designed to promote reflection on the
politics of one's organization. The dilemma of whose
ends/interests come first - those of the individual or those of
the organization - captures a central "political" tension.
Conflicts between individual and organizational goals lie at the
heart of much organizational politics! The exercise encourages
people to look for this tension in their own organization, and to
follow its implications. Links to COT #63 - Rational for whom?

PLURALIST MANAGEMENT (COT #95)

A simple exercise designed to get the student to think about
strategies of conflict management (important links with COT #s
59, 60, 61, 62). The questions posed in the exercise help to
create a focus through which the student can apply the ideas
identified in the readings.

MEETINGS, MEETINGS, MEETINGS (COT #96)

Another simple exercise designed to illustrate the political
tensions inherent in everyday decisions. The decision on what
meetings one plans to attend involve decisions about the power
and politics in one's organization, the consequence of one's
decision on the perceptions of others, the impact on career
prospects, etc..

SUNNYVALE YOUTH CENTRE (COT #96)

Overview

This case is excellent for illustrating the relationships
between culture and politics, especially in relation to the
formation of coalitions, and the role of impression
management/the management of meaning in power relations. The case
builds on the competing values and orientations represented by
two employees, Marg Johnson and Mike Thornton - archetypal
representatives of the way different professional orientations
can divide an organization.

Analysis

There are at least three possible explanations of this case, all
of which are inter-twined. A great case for illustrating the
premises of Images and how a comprehensive "reading" of the
Sunnyvale situation can open interesting action possibilities.
The three explanations are those of:

1. An organization in transition that has the problem of reconciling conflicting demands from its environment for business efficiency and a strong humanistic "client orientation". (This is typical of many social service organizations at the present time. The split is also found in other guises, especially bureaucratic-professional conflict, in organizations in all sectors of society). The case issues a classic warning to efficiency oriented business students, who are dominated by rational concepts of organization. Marg Johnson does the job for which she was appointed, but she is perceived as ineffective.

2. An organization that is locked in a destructive relationship between culture and counter-culture. There is a clear split in values between the efficiency and client orientations: "balanced budgets" vs the kids. It is played in the form of a conflict between the professional manager (and her allies) and the social workers and volunteers.

3. A case of organizational politics: are Thornton and Hubbard arch manipulators using the organization for their own ends? The case bristles with examples of outright manipulation, coalition building, and savvy use of new appointments, committees, etc. for a variety of ends. A special feature rests in how Thornton defines Marg's identity for the rest of the organization.

Strong evidence can be marshalled in favor of each interpretation. The skill in analysis rests in being able to get a grasp on these inter- twined relations, and to grasp which are the important driving forces. If the political motives are dominant, then there is probably little that can be done to bind the organization together. If they are secondary, a consequence of real fears about the conflicting demands of "efficiency" and "the kids", then they are open to some form of management.

To unravel the issues I like to begin the case with the question: How would you explain events at Sunnvdale? This invariably brings out all the above issues. They can then be counterposed as competing or related explanations. As each theme is identified, it can be explored in greater depth.

I then tie the case together asking: How could Marg Johnson have been more effective in her role as Executive Director? This typically adds sharper focus to the issues. A typical analysis usually identifies the following considerations.

(a) Marg could have "read" her role in a more informed manner. If she had appreciated the kids-oriented culture and its significance, she could have tempered her overly rational approach. She could have found ways of blending the pursuit of efficiency with a good deal for the kids. She could have tried to develop a situation where others make the hard decisions, being content to pose alternatives. She could have acted as a "broker" between rival stakeholders, trying to find acceptable rather than strictly rational solutions.

(b) She could have had a better appreciation of the symbolic side of management. In cutting the Glenbow Falls trip she attacked a strong symbol, undermining her credibility and making many enemies. She was unaware of the symbolic significance of seemingly "rational" aspects of organization. For example, the very idea of a balanced budget is often anathema to social service employees with a strong humanitarian and client orientation. For them Marg and her actions symbolized the problems facing the agency; she was seen as part of the problem, not the solution. She failed to appreciate this.

(c) Her passive attitude allowed others to define her role and personal image. For example, a strong case can be made for the idea that Marg's image in the organization was enacted (and systematically distorted?) by Thornton. He defines her identity as far as other employees are concerned. Thornton is skilled in the management of meaning and uses many complementary techniques e.g. stereotyping Johnson as the callous business manager, and as the "computer whiz" who is against the kids; he socializes new recruits with regard to Marg and her role; he uses the kid's cartoon (an idea planted by himself?) to entrench her image; he makes use of evocative language and imagery, and builds patterns of shared interpretation e.g. in his alliance with Mrs. Hubbard. Thornton seems to be a very skilled organizational politician and succeeds well in his task. Marg's passivity hands the whole situation to him more or less "on a plate".

(d) Marg herself could have become politically more active, building coalitions and an effective power base within the organization. Soon after her arrival she loses the key support of Mrs. Grant, and it is never replaced. She was an outsider and remained an outsider. The circumstances of her appointment reveal a split within the Board and organization, and she does nothing to recognize and deal with this, and related factors that emerge.

All in all, an awareness of the importance of culture and politics in an organizational context could have transformed Marg's role.

The case can thus be played in many ways, with different foci of interest. It is excellent for illustrating how cultures are enacted, the links between culture and politics, and for studying the detailed dynamics of organizational politics, especially with regard to the "management of meaning." The potential in this case for a fully developed political analysis is great.

CONFLICT AT RIVERSIDE (COT #98)

Overview:

An excellent case for illustrating the process of "reading" organizations, and how one's readings can shape actions. Very powerful illustration of the potential incompatibility of interests between labour and management, and of the political dilemmas this raises. Note the links with It's Not Working, discussed later in this manual.

Analysis:

1. This simple story illustrates a crucial feature of organizational life. Rod and Steve are talking about the same situation. But they have very different "readings" of that situation. For Steve the Company is in a critical stage of development, re-shaping itself to keep abreast of advances in technology, and to retain a competitive position in its wider environment. He tends to see the organization as a (potentially) unified entity attempting to survive in an evolving world. He believes that the people initiating the changes are doing an excellent job, and are trying hard to find a solution that will benefit everyone in the organization. He believes that the developments at the Riverside plant signify the march of progress, and should be readily implemented by all involved.

Rod, on the other hand, is more skeptical. He too recognizes that the developments may be crucial for the organization's survival, but interprets them in a context where some people are going to gain and others lose. Change, for him, is a two-edged sword, entailing loss of jobs, poorer career prospects, and the eventual demise of trade-union power within the company. For Rod there is also the strong suspicion that management are playing a clever political game, and that the offer of a sweet-deal at Riverside with short-term benefits disguises some of the longer-term consequences for workers in the company at large.

Of one thing we can be certain. The way Rod and Steve read their organization will influence how they act when they return to work on Monday. There is just a chance that the conversation has served to influence or change their points of view. If so, Steve may keep a closer watch on the politics of the Riverside project to see if Rod's suspicions hold. And Rod may try and take a second look at whether management is really interested in moving into a new era of collaboration with the workforce. And this may influence the stand that he will take in discussions with his fellow unionists.

If, on the other hand, both are unconvinced by the other's point of view, their original way of reading the situation is likely to be reinforced. Steve may feel that Rod, as he always suspected, is just a stubborn trade-unionist who is unable to understand the reality facing the company. And from Rod's point of view, the conversation may serve to reinforce his view that Steve is just another management lackey who is either being devious in pretending not to see the long-term consequences of the Riverside project (which, of course, may be the case) or who is just more naive than Rod originally thought. Steve, in Rod's view, may have just spouted the usual managerial rhetoric that confirms management's insensitivity to the basic needs and concerns of the work force. He will return to work on Monday as determined as ever to do whatever he can to squeeze the best possible deal for his members, even if it does hurt the future of the company.

This line of argument provides a platform for discussing issues relating to the enactment of organizational reality in politicized contexts, and the question of whether win/lose relations can be reframed.

2. The case also raises the question of whether organizations are unitary systems, or pluralist/radical systems. (Images Chapter 6)

How are we to make sense of the organization described in this case? Clearly, the nature and significance of the Riverside project - as a clue to the nature of the overall organization - can be "read" in different ways.

If we follow Steve's interpretation then we are encouraged to believe that his organization is a kind of organism attempting to survive in a competitive environment. The company is presented as being in a critical stage of development, and as having to meet the challenges of an evolving world. In Steve's view, the organization must act as a unified entity and evolve along with changing times, or die.

If we follow Rod's interpretation, on the other hand, we are encouraged to view the organization as being more like a political system. His view stresses the divisions within the organization, the fact that the proposed changes will benefit some organizational members while harming others, and that the Riverside project is underpinned by a hidden managerial agenda to undermine union power. The organization is viewed as an arena where different groups are struggling to advance or defend very different sets of interests.

Which of these interpretations is the more valid? Is one better than the other? Or could it be that both have something to tell us about this organization?

In order to answer these questions we would need to probe the background to the Riverside project in greater depth. We would need to test Steve's opinion that the management of the company are trying to take everyone's interests into account. And we would need to explore the evidence for Rod's view that management are playing a political game, and that their ultimate agenda is to break the union to gain full control over the workforce. There is room for an excellent class debate about this, leading into more general issues about labour-management relations, and the "radicalization" of organizations.

3. Finally, the case raises a major set of philosophical-political-ideological issues with regard to the very concept of "an organization". The main paradox illustrated in the Riverside case is evident in the question of whether it makes sense to talk about the organization surviving, as Steve does, if it means survival without the likes of Rod and his work-mates. The paradox hinges on whether the labour force are to be considered part of the organization. If so, then surely survival means that the labour force, albeit with an evolving role, must survive along with the rest of the organization. If not, then the organization is perhaps more accurately viewed through the eyes of Rod, as a battle-ground between competing sets of interest, e.g. of shareholders, managers, and the workforce. Or it requires a new "stakeholder view" of organization explicitly recognizing these different interest groups. This kind of paradox underpins many contemporary problems between labour and management, and arises not because one side or another is bloody-minded or out to create trouble, but because they find themselves caught in the kind of tension described above. Given cooperative attitudes on both sides that could produce a major restructuring of the company, even a labour-oriented management would find itself having to make decisions which create the kind of division between "us" (who have a future with the organization) and "them" (who don't). A great case for helping students appreciate the very real problems underpinning labour-management relations, and the contradictions shaping the organizational world.

THE HANDGRENADE (COT #99)

A straightforward case illustrating some manipulative political tactics. Steve Johns, the case narrator, lets us share his thinking. In the process we see how people's interpretations/enactment of the world around them help political dramas unfold. Steve is a nice guy, perhaps a little too obviously careerist, but ends up on the receiving end of a nasty political trick.

Use the case to initiate discussion about exactly how Machiavellian organizational life is in practice. (Note links with COT #s 58, 66). Make a lot of the enactment theme. Is Steve setting himself up for this kind of put down - he's obviously striving to get ahead?

JERSEY PACKERS (COT #100)

Overview

This case follows the short career of Cindy Wanstall in a meat packing firm. She has aspirations to be the first female brand manager in the industry and in her attempt to be successful, becomes embroiled in a good old case of career politics, flavored by various hints of sexual discrimination.

Analysis

A central question underlying this case is whether it is:

    a) A case of sexual discrimination, or
    b) A case of frustrating work and a mismatch between job opportunities and career aspirations in the context of a very traditional, male dominated, slow moving firm.

1. As might be expected in the meat packing industry, Wanstall encounters a lot of joking and mild harassment in relation to her role as a woman, but she survives it with accomplishment, soon being accepted as "one of the boys". However, things start to go wrong for Cindy as she begins to get frustrated with the nature of her work and the slow progress being made towards her career aims. An excellent class discussion can be generated by attempting to bring out opinions of the class in relation to these issues, creating a dialectic between those that hold the two different points of view. Many of the facts of the case are fuzzy, providing the basis for a lively argument.

2. One interpretation would place emphasis on the importance of a mismatch between task and career interests in setting

the context of all that happens. Cindy is in a job that
moves too slowly to meet her aspirations. She begins to get
quite frustrated, and her encounters with middle management,
particularly Rod Fuller, bring out a variety of issues in
relation to gender politics. Cindy's abrasive style
provokes Fuller into exposing his chauvinist bias through
various sexist comments. From this point in the case, the
situation escalates, day to day working relations between
Cindy and Fuller breaking down, the latter eventually
producing negative reports on her overall performance.
Cindy then has a weapon in her hand in that the report uses
the word emotional, a female stereotype, and perhaps the
beginnings of a harassment case.

3. The whole case thus raises gender issues. Cindy is a
woman in a man's world. But is she the aggressor? It is
she who raises the issue of discrimination, and begins to
use it for her own career ends.

4. The case thus hinges on this dialectic between progress
in an unsatisfactory job, and the issue of discrimination,
and they are intertwined. The "causal factors" - chauvinism
versus careerism - can be argued either way. Whatever your
view, use the case to explore the issue of gender politics,
focussing on the political skills that Cindy could have used
to improve her situation.

THE DEPARTMENT OF INFORMATION SERVICES (COT #101)

Overview

This is an excellent case for illustrating the difficulties that
bureaucracies often encounter in dealing with technical change,
and the way in which organizational politics influence this
process. The agency in question is the Information Services
Branch of the Regional Bureau of Administrative Affairs. It is a
highly bureaucratized department, working within a bureaucratized
context, providing information services to other agencies of the
Regional Government. The agency is experiencing difficulties in
dealing with the "micro" revolution. The routine of the
department, is disrupted by the arrival of a newcomer. She finds
it difficult to fit in, breaks all the informal rules of the
organization, and eventually leaves.

The case illustrates familiar conflicts between the old guard
and new guard, illustrating how an entrenched corporate culture
and associated politics can pervade everything that is done in an
organization.

Analysis

The case can be used to bring out the following points as part
of an emerging political analysis.

1. There is clearly an entrenched pattern of interests among
senior members of the department, such as Brill, Jitney and
Wells, with Cray going along with the way things are. These
problems seem to be motivated by a combination of task and
career interests, though their interpretation of the task
that needs to be performed by the agency is a very
conservative and slow moving one. They have a narrow concept
of the possibility of information services within the
department. This pattern of interests is supported by the
entrenched corporate culture and respect for bureaucratic
routine, which gives rise to the existence of a strong "old
guard".

2. The newcomer, Ms. Dun, also seems motivated by task and
career interests. But she has a much more aggressive view of
the task which needs to be performed, and clearly has a very
different sense of the mission and direction of the
department as a whole. As a newcomer, she clearly wants to
make an impact. Her actions stir up the status quo, and do
much to create a division with the "old guard".

3. The major power sources within the organization are
primarily bureaucratic, supported by the corporate culture
which reinforces and entrenches these values. The department
is run in accordance with the rules, Brill, the executive
director, calling all the shots. The main countervailing
source of power is the technocratic, i.e. knowledge of
microprocessing, and the computer revolution. The chief
holder of this power is Dun. Given the nature of this
organization and the corporate culture, technical expertise
accounts for little. The level of competence required seems
to be rather minimal. The organization is clearly not at the
cutting edge of developments, nor does it have to be,
allowing the bureaucratic values to squeeze out the
technocratic.

Cray, the other main actor in this case, is not in a strong
power position. His power has been undermined by
decentralization, and he is not a high status person in the
bureaucracy. This may account for his willingness to go
along with Dun in her attempt to create a new direction.

4. The case is important in illustrating the issue of
central vs decentralized control. The new technology
challenges traditional bureaucratic values in a major way,
since introduction of the new technology will require all
sorts of changes in this cozy department and the mindsets of

its managers. This is probably an important factor adding to the solidity of the old guard, who probably see all these new developments as challenging their power positions, and future careers within the department. They thus have every reason to try and keep a lid on the change, going slowly but in the right direction.

5. There are also the usual "unconscious" factors that may help explain the resistance to change.

6. It is also important to understand some of the infrastructural factors that define the stage of action, particularly the passive civil service climate, the fact that the organization is in a protected environment, and that technological change is not crucial. All these factors are critical in allowing bureaucratic rather than technocratic values to remain in ascendancy.

7. <u>Has Dun behaved appropriately?</u> How could she have behaved differently?

(a) She is rather clumsy in reading the power structure and gives the impression of being a brash newcomer charging in. Clearly, a more sensitive view of the politics of organization would help her appreciate the dominant bureaucratic culture, and that technical know-how has lower priority. In being more aware of the power base of the department, she would have had a much more appropriate reading of the situation from which to base her detailed actions.

(b) She builds a coalition with the least powerful member. Cray has already lost great influence in the department, and is in no position to be a powerful ally. If the nature of the department was such that the technological changes were perceived as critical to its success, there would have been an opportunity for a minor faction to receive and increase in power by developing this kind of coalition, provided that it was supplemented with appropriate action. But given the entrenched bureaucracy, there seems to be no way that Dun is providing an appropriate base for action within this organization. She could have built a different coalitional structure, perhaps by talking more directly with the hierarchy, and seeing what sort of leeway there was for getting allies.

(c) She could have been more tactical in the way she prepared reports and submitted them. For example, she could have done more to canvas support in advance of her proposals to seek opinion, etc.. The report that she produces with Cray has merit politically in that it seeks to integrate the different sets of interest by holding on to the "mainframe", thus giving Jitney, Brill and others a sense of the status quo - trying to get to the middle ground, rather than seeking for a perfect solution. But tactics, given the entrenched power relations, could have been improved.

(d) The situation is very difficult for a get-ahead person. For she has to change the environment in which she works. Most people with any ambition would get frustrated in this kind of organization and would leave, unless they want a cozy job. A condition of membership is that one plays the game. If Dun is truly motivated to get highly involved in the new technology, then she may have taken the wrong job.

QUALITY CO-OP (COT #102)

This case illustrates tensions and power plays found in many non-profit organizations. As Quality Co-op develops over a period of fifteen years, its original values, aims and aspirations become a contested terrain. Two distinct sub-cultures develop within the organization and become the basis of rival coalitions. The management of the Co-op becomes completely politicized as the groups struggle for power. The case illustrates the paradox facing many similar organizations founded on democratic values and a concern to build community: community and shared values become rocked and reshaped by the interplay between the changing values/interests and power bases of members.

The discussion questions at the end of the case provide a springboard for investigating these issues, and discussing some of the problems of non-profit organizations in more general terms.

WHO BUILDS THE DILLWORTH EXTENSION? (COT #103)

Overview

This case features career politics set within the context of a property development company that has certain anomalies in its Departmental structure. It illustrates the importance of coalitions, power relations and the political tactics that may be used in corporate life.

Analysis

1. The case can be taken in many directions. On the face of it the situation seems cut and dried: it is a case of career politics. Farley has seized an opportunity (perhaps he has been waiting a long time) to advance himself within the organization. He tries to take it. But Dell and Basker are able to form a coalition, and with clear and resolute tactics outmanoeuvre him.

Developing this theme, the case can be used to illustrate a number of important points:

i) An excellent illustration of career politics, highlighting:

(a) The way alliances build around mutual interests (e.g. those of Dell and Basker).

(b) How the corporate culture shapes the approach taken on key decisions, e.g. speed is essential. This ethos places considerable pressure on Snider to find a way of saying yes; and simultaneously it creates great opportunity - for himself, and potentially for Farley and Dell.

(c) The importance of opportunism: Farley sees the possibility of gaining an inside edge; Snider takes a gamble on this project: he's lucky it comes off!

(d) The anomalies that can arise from idiosyncracies in Departmental structure - the strange relationship between Development and Maintenance, and between Maintenance and Purchasing.

(ii) An excellent illustration of the use of power:

(a) The power arising from the ethos of "getting things done on time", i.e. there is a power relation in the request to Snider to investigate the job.

(b) The power arising from dependence, e.g. of Maintenance on Development's engineering staff; of Snider's dependence on Farley and Dell.

(c) The power reflected in the blocking and delaying tactics by the Purchasing department and from the ability to withhold information.

(d) The power associated with being "unavailable"; in this case Basker's absence.

(e) The power associated with developing a crucial coalition, and having a clear plan of action - Dell and Basker do a superb job in blocking Farley.

(f) The power plays associated with gender: Farley tries to use the fact that Dell is a woman, to undermine her status in conversation with Snider.
(g) The power of rules established by the head office: the restriction on the staffing of the Development department.

(iii) The case also illustrates general principles in relation to the rationality and irrationality of the organization: the case is driven by personal motives, yet produces results that are rational for the organization.

2. But there is another aspect to the case which also can be explored.

The obvious interpretation from the career politics standpoint is that Farley is the prime mover.

But is he?

Is it possible that this kind of conflict is being "engineered" by Snider to create a more competitive work situation? Or even by the company, because it likes to promote a cut and thrust atmosphere - it is after all a company where the main concern is to do things on time and on budget.

The case is inconclusive. But it is an excellent vehicle for discussion, and I find that a class will often raise these issues themselves. Here is a way that discussion often unfolds:

(i) The case illustrates the importance of coalitions and how one can develop one's advantage by advancing mutual interests.

(ii) Farley was the prime-mover and Snider the opportunist:

Farley has been wanting to redress the imbalance of power in relation to the Development Department. This is his chance and he grabs it.

Snider sees a great opportunity in Farley's proposal to get a second chance at getting a viable project and jumps on board.

(iii) Snider was the prime-mover. He's a manipulator. He uses Farley to put pressure on the system. He wants the best of both worlds.

(iv) This kind of competition is encouraged by the head office. The system of dual responsibilities in staff departments (to regional and head offices) helps them to promote this kind of competition.

Such ideas, whether or not true, help the class to stretch its imagination and see beneath the surface of the case. As discussion of the various possibilities progresses, it typically brings out a range of insights and detail, e.g:

(a) Farley is in a weak position; he knows he is dependent on Dell; his move to get the contract is one of desperation.

(b) Dell has ultimate control over Farley, and she knows it.

(c) The episode is a massive affirmation of the corporate culture - "on time; on budget"; it reproduces and rewards the corporate values.

There is no predicting which way the discussion will go or what points the class will see. But in my experience it results in a very rich analysis. As I bring the discussion points together in developing and integrating the case, I focus on:

(a) The question of whether the conflict is positive or negative for the corporation as a whole, e.g. it stimulates competition, it reinforces key values; but it is also manipulative and is possibly laying the basis for long term problems between Development and Maintenance.

(b) Should the company try and eliminate the conflict? An excellent platform to talk about how many organizations promote conflict between groups to stimulate innovation, and how the conflict can provide the basis for learning. But, on the negative side, the conflict in this case is insidious rather than open; people may not be aware of the rules; it is also wasteful in certain respects. The whole discussion can lead to an analysis of how conflict is used and promoted as a constructive source of innovation, e.g. in companies that have parallel teams working on the same projects.

(c) Should the company attempt to develop a team approach within the Division, perhaps by creating conflict between divisions? Discussion here opens the way to examining how conflict can be reshaped by changing structures, behaviors, or perceptions (See COT #60).

(d) All in all, the case can provide an excellent platform for a discussion of pluralist politics, and conflict management. (Links to COT #s 59, 60, 61, 62, 63).

THE LAKESIDE LITERARY MAGAZINE (COT #104)

Overview

A literary magazine that undergoes major changes as a result of the orientations of new board members. Illustrates the cultural and political factors that can transform the way an organization runs, and the direction it takes.

Analysis

Use the discussion questions at the end of the case - or the broad question: What happened at LLM? - to focus on the coalitions and power plays. Focus on the key role played by Helen McAdam. What sources of power does she use to advance her ends? Is she using the rules and a token respect for democracy to shape events? A twist to the case can be generated by asking whether it is Ashley, rather than McAdam, who is the prime mover? This will help to get a better understanding of the political dynamic, and help to generate an excellent discussion of coalition building, power behind the scenes, etc..

The case has similarities with Quality Co-op and the Upstage Theatre Company, and can be used to reinforce basic themes, or used as an alternative.

THE UPSTAGE THEATRE COMPANY (COT #105)

Overview

This is an excellent case for illustrating organizational politics in action, with a focus on coalition building and power plays.

Analysis

1. The case presents an excellent illustration of how task, career and extra-mural interests intertwine, and provide the basis for coalition- building. Buck's proposal advances his task and career aims, with the latter possibly in ascendancy. Carlisle and Ramsay support his proposal because it supports their own personal "extra-mural" aims and agendas as much as it advances those of the Upstage Theatre Company. Vickers, eventually "buys into" the program because he is promised a "slice of the action".

2. The case thus shows how organizations can be driven by hidden agendas that are "political" rather than purely rational. And it provides valuable illustrations of the kind of manoeuvering and lobbying that supports this kind of political activity.

The real insights hidden in this case emerge as one investigates the political styles adopted by the various actors. To try and raise these I often pose the question: Who's the really sophisticated political actor in this case? Carlisle is the obvious answer, and she is indeed an accomplished politician. But look also at Buck. Is he the master politician? Is he building on Carlisle's "extra-mural interests" (community image) and using these for his own career interests? Are his "hint"s to Carlisle a "foot in the water"; a "sounding out"; a clever "seeding" of his initiative. Is this decision to go forward with his proposal at the meeting a conscious political decision knowing that Carlisle is likely to be "on side". If so, he has commissioned the most important player in this case in support of his cause. Given the obvious careeristic implications of his proposal there is great merit in Buck getting someone to run with his proposal. Has he anticipated this, and chosen to get Carlisle to orchestrate its acceptance and implementation? Much can be learned about the subtle nature of organizational politics from this kind of investigation and of how the real political movers in a situation are not always playing the most obvious and blatant roles. Politics is often more like "fly fishing" than confrontation and open debate.

A focus on Carlisle's strategy and behaviour also highlights similar points. She is an accomplished "orchestrator". Note how she passes the project to Ramsay to make the running. Her decision to ask him for his comments before getting Vicker's reaction is crucial in establishing the credibility of the proposal. And, as discussed below, she uses many other techniques to advance the proposal towards a successful conclusion.

3. The case thus provides an important backdrop for the discussion of coalition-building, and how this occurs. Though no explicit attention is devoted to the activities outside the Board meeting, the case suggests that there is probably quite a bit of lobbying between Buck and Carlisle, and possibly Ramsay. This provides an excellent basis for a discussion of coalition-building in general terms, as well as in terms of the details illustrated in this case e.g. marshalling support on the basis of converging interests, getting people "onside", orchestrating outside a meeting and stage-managing within, etc..

4. The case has many illustrations relating to the use of power: Carlisle's clever use of her role as chairperson e.g. by looking to Ramsay rather than Vickers to initiate discussion, the coalition-building process, the use of "rationalizations" (in the form of financial and market surveys) to support decisions one favors, the use of voting rights and "one-third" minorities to stall progress etc.. Organizations are often rationalizing, not rational!

5. Assessments can also be made of the political styles of the actors involved, especially Buck, Carlisle and Vickers. What are the strengths and weaknesses of their approaches to decision-making? How could they have been more effective? What general lessons can be drawn about the power and politics of decision- making in general terms?

6. The case provides an excellent "partner" to the "Global" role play (COT #93). The latter illustrates the inter-personal dynamics found in the Upstage Theatre Company in a very real way. The case thus presents an excellent platform for generalizing the insights that can be drawn from the role-plays.

7. Get students to link this case to their experience of meetings generally. To what extent do the politics of their organization follow a similar pattern?

TIPDALE ENGINEERING (COT #106)

Overview

A case featuring the development of a company where the visionary, dynamic entrepreneur David Tipdale "can't let go" and allow a new mode of operation emerge. The case features clashing visions, power struggles between Tipdale and his board, and with his newly appointed Executive V-P, and various political manoeuvres designed to retain control.

Analysis

The case can be used to highlight a number of important points:

1. The links with the life-cycle theory of organization (COT #38)

2. The role of the leader in shaping key values and overall direction of the organization.

3. The cleavages that can occur within the top coalition- note the links with Apple Computer (COT #57 and the casenotes in this manual).

4. The detailed power plays that Tipdale uses to retain control, and those used by his main "adversaries" - Larkin and Danson.

An excellent case for illustrating the politics of organization and how the fate of the whole may depend on very basic struggles for control.

PROBLEMS IN THE MACHINE SHOP (COT #107)

Overview

This is an excellent case for illustrating the problems of conflict and conflict management in manufacturing firms that are divided along class lines. Excellent as a bridge between discussions of pluralist politics and the radical frame of reference.

The case focuses on the experience of Jim Biltmore, a young engineer, recently graduated as an MBA, who has accepted a job as manager of a machine shop. He has decided to exercise his formal authority by writing instructions to two senior machinists, many years older and much more experienced than himself. He has received no reply, and is wondering what to do.

The class is asked to advise him.

Analysis

1. The basic problem is easy to spot. Jim has tried to exercise his formal authority, and it is vacuous. The men on the floor have the real power. Jim is dependent on them and they know it. The men's actions are sending him a clear message: he is a greenhorn and doesn't have any clout. Many members of class are often able to recall similarexperiences.

2. The case provides an excellent illustration of the difference between power and authority, and how authority has to be legitimated from below.

3. The case also provides a nice illustration of a degradation ritual that serves to equalize power relations.

4. The case is extremely valuable when used to identify and discuss the possible strategies that Biltmore can use in relation to his situation. Here is a list that is often identified in class discussion:

(a) Be humble and try to "save face".

(b) Find out what Jim can do for them, i.e. develop dependencies.

(c) Try and build friendship/alliances; must be genuine or it will be seen as manipulative.

(d) Spend time listening to the issues that are important to his staff and then try and build on their needs.

(e) Put them in charge (initially) and let them help him.

(f) Pretend nothing has happened - don't hide - get out there in the background and try and let the incident get into background.

(g) Confront them: directly or with another means.

(h) Try and create conflict within the workplace to divide and rule.

Of these (g) and (h) are likely to prove disastrous. Combinations of (a) and (f) may be more promising, especially if the problem of being manipulative, or leaving the work-group in full control, can be avoided.

(5) A deeper analysis suggests that Biltmore should:

(a) Try and understand what has happened:

- He has tried to use power he doesn't really have.

- The workforce are in control and they know it.

- If he tries to force his position, he can create further difficulties; they can continue to make his life difficult; let him down on crucial occasions; and even put him in a situation where he will end up getting fired.

- He has built a coalition against himself.

- He has created a story that will enter the organization's culture.

- His action is probably born of insecurity - e.g. the fact that as a manager he feels he should be "managing" and "on top of things".

(b) The only strategy he really has open is to acknowledge to himself that he has made a mistake, and try to recoup the situation as best as he can. Manipulative strategies will surely be seen as game playing, and will generate further manipulation as a response. It is a game that Biltmore can't win.

(c) Whether Biltmore will be successful in developing good relations with the workforce will ultimately depend on the history underlying the situation. If the organization is deeply radicalized on an "us and them" basis, it is unlikely that he can produce more than temporary "band-aid" solutions. He may be on the front-line of an ongoing battle, and powerless to win. In this case he can only survive as best he can. If he gets too close to the workers, he will become suspect from a managerial point of view; and if he stays close to management, he will always be an outsider on the shop floor. If the episode just has symbolic significance in the sense of telling Biltmore to "know your place young man" and "show respect", then he may be able to regain ground.

(6) The case is excellent for providing a link between discussion of pluralistic politics and the radical frame of reference (Note COT #s 62, 66, 95, 98). It shows that some conflict is deeply embedded in values and attitudes and cannot easily be reconciled. Ideal as a platform for systematic examination of the radical frame of reference in subsequent classes.

(7) The case often generates many stories and real-life experiences from the class, e.g. of the upstart engineer who established bad relations with his workforce. One day the factory began to flood. There was a valve to shut off the water, well known to the men, but of which the engineer wasn't aware. On instructions to the men "do something!", they brought him a boat. He was fired the following day!

VISIBILITY, AUTONOMY, RELEVANCE AND RELATIONSHIPS (COT #108)

This questionnaire, devised by Rosabeth Moss Kanter and her colleagues at Goodmeasure, creates an excellent opportunity for people to analyze power relations with a personal focus.

Use the results as a basis for class discussion

DEBATE: PROFIT AND ORGANIZATIONS - A STORY OF EXPLOITATION? (COT #109)

The questions providing a focus for this debate are presented in COT #109.

Vic Murray of York University designed this exercise and suggests the following arrangements:

Create Four Groups

Debate Format: 20 mins. to prepare both topics and choose debaters.

Presentation: 5 mins. (maximum) for each side plus 2 minutes rebuttal.

Class vote on each issue.

Topic Allocation:

Issue

	1		2		3		4	
	A	N	A	N	A	N	A	N
Group 1	X		X					
2		X	X					
3				X				X
4					X	X		

A = Affirmative

B = Negative

1e, group # 1 will take on affirmative on issue #1 & a negative on issue #2.

group #2 a negative on #1 & affirmative on #2.

Use the debate to bring out conflicting views of organization. The exercise provides an excellent supplement to COT #s 56, 70, 71, 72, 98; also see It's Not Working, discussed in the next section of these notes.

The links between the debate and most of these other COT items are obvious, e.g. the Bhopal disaster - but those with COT # 70, The Destructive Side of Technological Development, are worthy of special mention. In this resource item John Mcknight provides a critique of technology itself, showing how its very use (even when it seems neutral or beneficial) can have major systemic consequences. The article illustrates what Gregory Bateson (Steps To An Ecology of Mind, 1972) would describe as the pathologies of conscious purpose. The article can be used to provoke discussion on many controversial topics, e.g. does the medical profession institutionalize ill-health? Does the educational profession institutionalize passivity? Does counselling institutionalize dependence? The questions imply extreme points of view - like the questions in the debate. But they can be used to stimulate thinking about these and other important issues.

IT'S NOT WORKING

Overview

This video (taken from the PBS programme Bill Moyer's Journal) focuses on the closure of the U.S. Steel plant at Youngstown Ohio. I use the extracts focusing on community and labor reactions to the closure. The video presents a very lively meeting at which union members hear speakers and offer their own views on what can be done. A classic illustration of the radicalization of the work-place, and of the radical frame of reference (The video also contains useful footage on the exploration of various forms of workers' control, of relevance to classes on both the political and domination metaphors.)

Analysis

I use the case to illustrate the antagonistic relations that often exist between the interests of workers and their organizations and the radical frame of reference in practice - a useful visual illustration of some of the tensions presented in Conflict at Riverside (COT #98).

To initiate discussion I use the following lead questions:

1. What are the main issues raised by this case? followed by questions such as:

2. Do you think that most organizations are run in favor of the interests of capital and against those of labor?

3. Are there implications of the Youngstown experience for the way organizations are designed and managed in the future?

4. Do you think that there is any way of getting beyond the labor-management split? If so, how?

The whole purpose of the video is to illustrate the exploitative side of organizational life, and bring out the union/labor standpoint in full force. The video is a powerful means of doing this. It allows management students to see organizations from "the other side" and to grasp the kind of anger that radicalizes so many organizations.

There is no way of predicting class reactions. Sometimes they are ultra conservative: "It's all the union's fault". Sometimes they're sympathetic. My lead question brings out a range of opinions and provides a foundation for debate. Typically, the following issues are raised:

(a) The video illustrates the importance of the social responsibility of business: workers depend on organizations for their livelihood.

(b) The video reflects the march of progress. Some plants and business have to die. Workers have to learn to change with the times.

(c) Businesses are usually interested in profits and little else. The video illustrates the fundamental divisions found in many organizations e.g., people vs. money, labor vs. capital, unions vs. management, "us" vs. "them".

(d) Business schools are interested in money issues, not people issues. They are ideological training grounds serving the interests of capital.

(e) The video illustrates the ultimate powerlessness of labor. Though unions were strong in the 1960's and 1970's they may have had their day. Ultimate power rests with capital.

And so on.

In drawing out a range of opinion it is possible to create a debate between those holding rival points of view. In the process, it is possible to identify and develop the distinctions between the "radical" and the "pluralist" frames of reference, to cultivate an understanding of the nature of "radicalized organizations"; to illustrate how power relations may rest in the deep structure of a society (in the stage of action) rather than in more superficial sources. The case provides an excellent platform on which to build an exposition of Marxian economic theory, and the importance of understanding the logic of change shaping organizations and society (see Chapter 8 of Images for an exposition).

FINAL OFFER (COT #110)

A great video for illustrating deep divides between management and labor, and the strategies and tactics that shape union politics, and the negotiations between unions and management. It's so rich that I can only advise you to watch the whole video and decide which sections you'd like to use. It will be well worth your time.

V. ENDNOTE

By way of closure, I hope that you will find these notes valuable
in conducting your courses. One of my aims in writing COT and
this manual is to set the basis for a wider system of exchange
between colleagues interested in the general approach. I will
thus be delighted to receive any ideas or comments that you wish
to make, and to hear of any cases, readings, videos or other
materials that would enrich future editions. So please feel free
to write, or just to send a copy of your course outline, so that
I can see which readings and cases in COT seem most valuable.

In the meantime, good luck with the ideas and materials.

Gareth Morgan
Faculty of Administrative Studies
York University
4700 Keele Street
Toronto, Canada M3J 1P3

NOTES

NOTES

NOTES

NOTES

NOTES

NOTES